TOLERATING ABUSES
VIOLATIONS OF HUMAN RIGHTS IN PERU

An Americas Watch Report

October 1988

36 W. 44th Street
New York, NY 10036
(212) 840-9460

739 Eighth Street, S.E.
Washington, DC 20003
(202) 546-9336

THE AMERICAS WATCH COMMITTEE

The Americas Watch Committee was established in 1981 to monitor and promote observance of free expression and other internationally recognized human rights in Central America, South America and the Caribbean. The Chairman of Americas Watch is Adrian W. DeWind; Vice Chairmen, Aryeh Neier and Stephen Kass; Washington Office Director, Juan E. Mendez; Associate Director, Cynthia Brown; Reports Editor, Anne Manuel; Counsel, Jemera Rone.

HUMAN RIGHTS WATCH

Human Rights Watch is composed of three Watch Committees: Americas Watch, Asia Watch and Helsinki Watch.

Executive Committee: Robert L. Bernstein (Chairman); Adrian W. DeWind (Vice Chairman); Roland Algrant; Dorothy Cullman; Jack Greenberg; Alice H. Henkin; Stephen Kass; Jeri Laber*; Aryeh Neier*; Matthew Nimetz; Bruce Rabb; Kenneth Roth.*

　　　　*ex officio

Staff: Executive Director, Aryeh Neier; Deputy Director, Kenneth Roth; Washington Representative, Holly J. Burkhalter; Special Projects Director, Wendy Luers; Press Director, Susan Osnos; Case Work Coordinator, Joanna Weschler.

Copies of this report are available for $6.00 from:

Human Rights Watch

36 West 44th Street	739 Eighth Street, S.E.
New York, NY 10036	Washington, DC 20003
(212) 840-9460	(202) 546-9336

Table of Contents

I.	PREFACE 1	
II.	SUMMARY AND RECOMMENDATIONS 3	
III.	THE DIFFICULTIES OF PERUVIAN DEMOCRACY 11	
IV.	VIOLATIONS OF THE LAWS OF WAR COMMITTED BY INSURGENTS . . 15	
V.	THE LEGAL AND MILITARY ASPECTS OF THE GOVERNMENT'S COUNTER-INSURGENCY STRATEGY 23	

	A.	The State of Emergency 23
	B.	Anti-Terrorist Legislation 26
	C.	Administration of Justice 33
	D.	The Military's Counter-Insurgency Strategy 36

VI.	HUMAN RIGHTS VIOLATIONS IN 1987 AND 1988 41	

	A.	Disappearances 41
	B.	Torture 46
	C.	Extra-Judicial Executions 50
		1. Executions by the Military 50
		2. Executions by the Comando Rodrigo Franco 53

VII.	FREEDOM OF EXPRESSION 57	
VIII.	RESTRICTIONS ON HUMAN RIGHTS AND HUMANITARIAN ORGANIZATIONS 59	
IX.	THE ROLE OF OTHER BRANCHES OF GOVERNMENT IN PROTECTING HUMAN RIGHTS 63	

	A.	Congress 63
		1. The Ames Commission 63
		2. The Melgar Commission 67
	B.	The Judiciary 70
	C.	The Office of the Prosecutor General 72

X.	THE ROLE OF THE UNITED STATES 77	
XI.	RECAPITULATION: WHY ARE HUMAN RIGHTS VIOLATED IN PERU? . 81	

	A.	The Split Between State and Society 81
	B.	Counter-Insurgency Strategy 82
	C.	The Attitude of the Insurgent Groups 82
	D.	The Weakness of the Judicial System 83
	E.	The Lack of Political Will on the Part of Civilian Governments Since 1980 83
	F.	The Lack of Mobilization of the Citizenry 84

APPENDIX

I. PREFACE

Since 1983, Americas Watch has followed the situation of human rights in Peru with increasing concern, and has periodically published reports on the subject. Except for the first report (*Abdicating Democratic Authority,* New York, 1984), all focused on the government of President Alan García, which was elected in 1985 with a broad popular mandate. In particular, our reports addressed the struggle against political violence and the need to control the government's own forces so as to prevent abuses of human rights. Each of those reports was the result of research missions to Peru by Americas Watch. Since 1985 each of our reports has been published in both English and Spanish, with the invaluable assistance of the Andean Commission of Jurists in producing the Spanish-language versions.

The current report is based, for the most part, on information gathered during a mission to Peru conducted in July 1988 by Juan E. Méndez, Director of the Washington Office of Americas Watch. In Peru, Mr. Méndez was joined by Sonia Goldenberg, a consultant to Americas Watch. The Americas Watch researchers enjoyed broad cooperation from the Peruvian authorities, with the exception of the Political-Military Command of Ayacucho, which expelled Mr. Méndez from the so-called "zone of emergency," as described in detail in a later section of this report. In Lima, Americas Watch interviewed Prime Minister Armando Villanueva, Minister of Justice Camilo Carrillo, Minister of Interior Admiral Juan Soria and Foreign Minister Luis Gonzales Posada. In addition, Americas Watch met with the Director of the Investigations Police (PIP), General Fernando Reyes Roca; the Attorney General (*Fiscal de la Nación*), Dr. Hugo Denegri; the President of the Senate, Jorge Lozada Stambury; and members of the Peruvian Congress from all parties. The discussions were frank and productive, but our request to visit the facilities of the police Directorate Against Terrorism (DIRCOTE) was ultimately not granted, nor have we received, as of the publication of this report, any answer to the letter we

1

addressed to President García on July 11, 1988 regarding our expulsion from the zone of emergency. The text of that letter, which was publicized at that time in the Peruvian press, is reprinted in the appendix.

In the course of our visit, as during our previous visits to Peru, we also met with journalists, local authorities, researchers, political analysts and representatives of Peruvian and international relief organizations. In addition, we received the generous cooperation of our colleagues in the human rights movement of Peru, a cooperation that extends far beyond our actual visit and reflects a continuing relationship with each of the organizations involved in that movement. We express our gratitude to our friends in the Andean Commission of Jurists (CAJ), the Center of Studies and Action for Peace (CEAPAZ), the Legal Defense Institute (IDL), the Bishops' Commission for Social Action (CEAS), the National Coordinating Body for Human Rights, the Association for Human Rights (APRODEH) and the Human Rights Commission (COMISEDH, formerly known as CONADEH).

This report was written by Mr. Méndez and Carlos Chipoco Cáceda of our Washington office. Sonia Goldenberg contributed to the research; worked with us, as noted above, during our visit to Peru in July 1988; and provided comments and suggestions for the text of this report. Once again, the Spanish version is published with the assistance of the Andean Commission of Jurists.

II. SUMMARY AND RECOMMENDATIONS

Peru is going through a particularly difficult period. Since 1980, when the Maoist extremist group *Sendero Luminoso* (Shining Path) initiated its armed confrontation with the democratically elected government, lethal violence has spread throughout the country. The victims of political violence number in the thousands. Together with Colombia, Peru now has the sad privilege to be counted among the most violent and dangerous places in South America.

In the early 1980s, the civilian authorities of this democracy, then emerging from a long period of military dictatorship, failed to affirm democratic authority over the military. Instead, civilian leaders tolerated the human rights violations which sectors of the security forces asserted to be a necessary concomitant of war.

President Alan García had an excellent opportunity to break with this approach. He enjoyed unprecedented popularity and legitimacy after winning the 1985 elections with close to 50% of the vote, and he belonged to a political party that had been an outspoken critic of the human rights policy of his predecessor, President Fernando Belaúnde. Fundamental change was thus expected from President García, including the inauguration of an era of full respect for fundamental freedoms.

These expectations have not been fulfilled. After three years in power, President García's reputation has faded considerably, and the human rights situation has not substantially improved.

Since the civilian government was first confronted by armed attacks and terrorism, it has come under pressure from the security forces to invoke ever harsher and more severe counter-insurgency measures, based on the premise that the war against the insurgents is subject to no rules. The result has been a cascade of extrajudicial executions, arbitrary arrests, disappearances

3

and torture — not as mistakes or exceptional episodes in the counter-insurgency war, but as among its central features.

There has been virtually no democratic control of the government forces responsible for confronting the insurgent groups. A commission of the Peruvian Senate recently concluded that there is no coordination between the different sectors conducting the fighting and that they lack an integrated counter-insurgency strategy. The Ministry of Interior made similar findings.*
This lack of coordination is seen by many as the main reason for the failure of the government forces to quell the insurgency.

Another key factor, however, has been the continuing violation of basic rights, particularly in the extremely poor emergency zones. Those violations have exacerbated a situation in which the local population feels no identification with government forces, and thus provides little assistance to government efforts to detect and root out the insurgents. The increasing insurgent presence, with a concomitant increase in assassinations and other terrorist actions, is thus, at least in part, the unfortunate and inevitable result of the maintenance of a policy that assigns no value to human rights.

Sendero Luminoso, for its part, has continued to commit murder and other violations of the laws of war as a deliberate part of its strategy. This self-styled Maoist group uses terror tactics to radicalize social conflict and to pitch rural communities against each other. It murders elected or appointed local officials as well as anyone it believes to be cooperating with the security forces or not cooperating sufficiently with the insurgency. In condemning this strategy, the Catholic Bishops of the Andean South have said:

> The groups that have taken up arms do not constitute any solution to the situation of structural violence. In fact, the type of action they perform destroys what the people have been building in the last few years as development alternatives. The messianic and authoritarian methods of this group, as well as the deaths they cause and murders they commit, cannot be justified under any circumstance. There is no life project in the

---

* Senate of the Republic of Peru, Special Commission on the Causes of Violence and Peace Alternatives, General Recommendations, p.10, Lima, July 1988.

massacres and crimes they conduct, nor in their destruction of the property and goods of the poorest among us. The popular alternative has nothing to do with intolerance or with the anti-democratic practices of these groups that attempt to grab its representation.*

The Movimiento Revolucionario Tupac Amaru (MRTA) also commits acts of violence, although it lacks the aggressiveness and dogmatism of Sendero Luminoso. MRTA has been responsible for serious violations of the rights of civilians and of the laws of war. The presence of one of its columns in San Martin, a department in the Peruvian jungle, caused a great stir in the latter part of 1987, but the group has now become less active and thus has receded in importance in comparison to Sendero. MRTA is similar to other Latin American guerrilla groups in that it tries to spark widespread rebellion, while Sendero's strategy is to generate a peasant rebellion against the cities. One of the alleged leaders of MRTA has characterized Sendero Luminoso's ideology as "a folk version of Maoism," while acknowledging that at least one military confrontation between the two groups has occurred.**

In the period covered by this report there was a significant increase in the most serious violations of human rights and the laws of war:

- The military's practice of causing forced disappearances has continued, primarily in the Ayacucho emergency zone. Public complaints and, most important, the role played by the *Fiscalía* in that region have secured the "re-appearance" of a large number of victims; nonetheless, the practice of causing the temporary or permanent disappearance of those suspected of activities in support of Sendero Luminoso has continued to be a deliberate and systematic policy of the security forces acting under the operational control of the Political-Military Command of Ayacucho. The number of registered complaints of disappearances rose in the course of 1988, particularly in June.

---

*   "We are still on time," Statement by the Bishops of the Andean South of Peru, Informativo Signos, Lima, July 1988.

**   Caretas, August 15, 1988.

5

- The Army has committed additional massacres of peasants in the emergency zone. The most notorious was the atrocious murder of 29 residents of the village of Cayara, Ayacucho, on May 14, 1988. The Army and the Government have tried, unconvincingly, to blame the episode on Sendero Luminoso, but the investigations that have taken place (despite interference by the Political-Military Command of Ayacucho) clearly demonstrate the military's responsibility.

- The insurgent groups, especially Sendero Luminoso, continue to engage in a deliberate practice of selective murders, in both the countryside and the cities. They also continue to place explosives in public places and to attempt to enlist the collaboration of civilians through intimidation.

- Torture at the hands of security forces remains a regular method for interrogating all detainees — those suspected of terrorism as well of those suspected of common offenses.

- The Government has restricted the work of the International Committee of the Red Cross (ICRC). Its delegates have no access to military detention centers in rural areas, nor, in Lima, to the facilities of DIRCOTE. Moreover, the Political-Military Command of Ayacucho has recently prohibited access to the area by the ICRC and other humanitarian organizations (*Medecins du Monde, Medecins sans Frontieres* and the Office of Social Assistance of the Archdiocese of Ayacucho). These organizations had been providing medical and emergency services to the rural population that had been displaced or otherwise affected by the war.

- A paramilitary group calling itself "Comando Rodrigo Franco" has begun to operate in recent weeks. It murdered a well known lawyer, Manuel Febres, who had defended prisoners accused of terrorist activity; exploded the tomb of a young woman who had been a member of Sendero in Ayacucho; and threatened to kill the special prosecutor who has been commissioned to investigate disappearances and the Cayara massacre.

- The government has conducted no serious investigation into the murder of the lawyer Manuel Febres, or the other crimes that have been committed against members of the Association of Democratic Lawyers in previous years, such as the disappearance of attorney José Vázquez Huayca in 1986 and other incidents described in the Americas Watch report on Peru in 1987.

- Representatives of highly regarded human rights organizations were detained at the order of the Ayacucho Political-Military Command, without the slightest justification. This episode in July was the first of its kind in recent years. A priest and three lay social workers, who formed a delegation from the Bishops' Commission on Social Actions (CEAS, the official Catholic Church agency that monitors human rights), were arrested and held in Ayacucho for about 30 hours. Two members of the Ayacucho office of the Service for Peace and Justice (SERPAJ), another Catholic group, received the same treatment.

- The military authorities of the emergency zone have continued their practice of prohibiting access by journalists to the rural areas of the region. In July, they took similar action against Americas Watch: Juan E. Méndez was prevented from travelling to the city of Huanta and ordered to return to Lima without completing his visit to Ayacucho.

- President García has introduced bills in Congress to revise the procedural and substantive criminal laws that apply to those accused of terrorism. If passed, these will severely limit due process guarantees and will end safeguards for the physical integrity of detainees that had been introduced just a year previously.

- Military jurisdiction continues to be the pretext for the effective impunity enjoyed by all members of the armed forces who commit human rights violations. To a lesser degree, the same is true for abuses committed by the police. Nonetheless, the formal prosecution submitted to the Supreme Council of the Armed Forces for the massacre in the Lurigancho penitentiary in June 1986, which was filed in July 1988, raises the hope that the murder of the hundreds of detainees who rioted in that prison will not continue to go unpunished.

- The various branches of government have continued to exhibit a passive attitude in the face of human rights violations, with honorable but rare exceptions. The perception that the judiciary is ineffectual in punishing terrorist offenses has grown in the public eye, thereby lending justification to those who advocate summary and illegal methods. The judiciary is also ineffectual in controlling abuses of authority. The standing committees of Congress concerned with human rights, and the special commissions of inquiry formed to investigate events such as those of the Cayara massacre, have been controlled by legislators of the ruling party who have not only refused to investigate the serious allegations but in some cases also have participated in cover-up activities.

- In this bleak picture there are two bright spots that must be noted:

   1.) the *Fiscal de la Nación* (attorney general) has appointed a special "commissioner," or prosecutor, to investigate disappearances in the emergency zone, Carlos Escobar Pineda. With strong support from the *Fiscal de la Nación* and the *Fiscal Supremo en lo Penal* (the chief prosecutor), Escobar has undertaken an investigative effort that is unique in its effectiveness, despite the serious personal risks he faces; and

   2.) the Commission of Inquiry into the prison massacres in Lima and Callao on June 18 and 19, 1986, chaired by Senator Rolando Ames, conducted a serious and searching investigation into this most bloody episode in recent Peruvian history, and produced a revealing and carefully documented report on the unfolding of the tragic events.

Americas Watch is deeply disappointed that the attitude of the government of President Alan García toward these problems has changed for the worse since he took office in 1985. In the early days of his tenure, the President decisively confronted the massacre by the Army of civilians in Accomarca by ordering immediate investigations and insisting on the removal of high-ranking Army officers who refused to cooperate with those investigations. In this manner, President García conveyed the impression that he was exercising his authority over the forces under his command and that he would not tolerate additional violations, even if the very serious abuses that had taken place under President Belaúnde were not investigated. Later, however, as our reports of 1986 and 1987 noted, the government adopted a certain passivity toward military abuses, although there were some more positive as well as negative signs.

Unfortunately, in 1988 that passivity has given way to apparent acquiescence, reflecting what seems to be a perception that abuses are inevitable. The attitude of the civilian government might best be described as one of resignation. Although every government official we interviewed asserted his intention to enforce the laws, we also found a tendency to accept and to repeat the explanations given by military authorities for violent deaths, even when those explanations were manifestly indefensible. Announcements that investigations will take place are now made only after the pressure of public opinion becomes irresistible, and the investigations are usually preceded or accompanied by expressions of support for the Armed Forces that sound like *a priori* exculpations. Impunity for those who wear uniforms continues, and the Peruvian public no longer believes that the government has any real intention of pursuing justice.

To be fair, it must be acknowledged that certain opposition sectors and influential communications media share in this tacit acceptance of human rights violations as the inevitable price to pay for combatting Sendero. In this way, the prevailing opinion in broad sectors of society contributes to the legitimation of the crimes committed by the authorities. It is the government, however, that bears the principal responsibility for this lack of ethical leadership. Its failure to exercise its authority to curb military abuses has been the key factor in producing the public attitude of acquiescence that we describe. It could well produce a further increase in the frequency of abuses as moral and institutional restraints are discarded, particularly as the activities of Sendero grow in intensity and criminality.

The government of President Fernando Belaúnde (1980-85) made a conscious decision to abdicate its authority over the military. It gave the military free rein to repress terrorism without legal or ethical constraints. What is worse, it covered up human rights violations and attacked foreign and domestic observers who pointed them out. In the view of Americas Watch, President Alan García has not descended to this level, nor can it be said that civilian authorities participate actively in illegal repression. But the government's tolerance of gross abuses of human rights is more and more apparent. The civilian government must be held accountable for this inaction and complacency, and for its acquiescence in the serious crimes committed by the armed forces in the name of defending the democratic system.

9

III. THE DIFFICULTIES OF PERUVIAN DEMOCRACY

Democracy in Peru was achieved in 1980 after more than eleven years of military dictatorship. The new 1979 Constitution provides detailed safeguards for human rights, a democratic system founded on genuine competition among diverse political parties, and a significant division of power among different branches of government and between central and regional authorities.

This young democracy, however, has had to face enormous problems during the tenures of its first two presidents. The most serious difficulty has been the prolonged economic crisis in which Peru is immersed. In 1985, annual per capita income was US$1,055, one of the lowest in Latin America.* The mortality rate for children under one year of age is 94 per thousand** — higher than the rate for Burma, Zambia, Guatemala, Ecuador, Colombia or Paraguay — and it is estimated to be still higher in rural areas like Ayacucho. In December 1987, the Peruvian foreign debt surpassed US$15 billion, after increasing 5.3% in 1986 and 6.9% in 1987. These rates of increase are higher than the overall rate for Latin America.***

Prospects for the immediate future are grim. Inflation has steadily increased this year: it was 30% in August and a record 130% in September. The

---

*   In South America, only Bolivia has a lower income per capita. Inter-American Development Bank figures, 1986.

**   World Development Report, 1987; World Bank, Washington.

***   Iguiñiz, Javier, Posición Peruana sobre la Deuda Externa: Experiencia y Lecciones, mimeo, Lima, 1988.

most optimistic estimates place the inflation rate for 1988 at over 1,000%.* Decreasing real wages, rising unemployment and underemployment, and deepening budget deficits have become increasingly familiar features of the Peruvian landscape.** All of this has accelerated a social crisis that began in the 1970's. Millions have moved to the poor suburbs of Lima and other cities, where they have demanded improved living conditions, including decent housing, water, health and food. Neither the democratic administration of Alan García nor that of his predecessor, Fernando Belaúnde, has been able to meet these needs.

In recent years there has been a noticeable increase in violence. Although violence has always been part of Peruvian history, the extremes reached in recent years constitute a new phenomenon, one that is virtually unprecedented throughout Latin America. Violence at the hands of terrorist groups and the military has been joined by an increase in common crime, particularly by gangs of drug traffickers in the Peruvian jungles. Peruvian officials cite over 10,000 deaths by political violence since 1980; human rights organizations place that figure at around 15,000. The majority of the victims have been innocent civilians, many of them children.

Insurgent groups, namely the Communist Party of Peru-"Sendero Luminoso" and the Movimiento Revolucionario Tupac Amaru (MRTA), carry a heavy burden of responsibility for this spiraling violence. Sendero unleashed its armed struggle precisely at the time when the country was starting on its path of constitutional democracy, a time when legal avenues for the pursuit of social and political change were wide open. The MRTA has also often shown a preference for violent over democratic change.

---

*   In September, the government adopted a package of economic measures that increased prices across the board, causing an overnight 50% reduction in purchasing power. In reaction, protests broke out in several cities, at times accompanied by looting.

**   Salaries have been falling abruptly since late 1987. Between November 1987 and April 1988, the average national salary lost 23.1% of its purchasing power, the legal minimum salary fell 20.1% and the salary of civil servants declined 30%. Employment levels have also been falling since the first quarter of 1988 (Iguiñiz, ob. cit., pg. 4).

Peruvian democracy has had to confront this explosive political violence. Unfortunately, the State has added to the violence by employing undemocratic and illegal means of repression. In this fashion, the loss of legitimacy that the state has suffered by its failure to respond to basic economic needs has been compounded by the illegitimate and violent methods used by its police and armed forces, often with the tolerance or acquiescence of elected officials.

There have been rumors that the military might attempt to interrupt the democratic process, fueled by statements made by high-ranking retired Army officers.* And in recent weeks, both the Prime Minister and the Minister of Defense have made statements denying rumors of coup attempts. In this regard, Americas Watch wants to make clear that, despite the enormous problems described in this report, a continuing democratic process in Peru is the only way to secure greater respect for human rights. It is, as well, the only way in which Peruvians can find civilized and fair solutions to their seemingly insurmountable problems.

Periodic elections force governments to respect a minimum legal order, if for no other reason than to maintain some degree of popularity. Those minimum legal standards are the only barrier between the present dramatic abuses and a bloodbath in which the absence of any limitations could cause the death of thousands. In a positive sense, as well, democracy provides the framework for the development of a national consensus on the way to address the fundamental problems confronting Peru.

A suspension of the constitutional process would indeed be tragic for human rights in Peru. Americas Watch calls on international public opinion to condemn, in clear and unmistakable terms, any movement toward a *coup d'etat*.

---

* See, for example, statements by General Luis Cisneros Vizquerra, <u>Caretas</u>, July 25, 1988, and retired General and former President Francisco Morales Bermudez, <u>Caretas</u>, October 17, 1988.

13

IV. VIOLATIONS OF THE LAWS OF WAR COMMITTED BY THE INSURGENTS

Sendero Luminoso systematically murders defenseless people, places explosives that cause great damage and endanger the lives of innocent bystanders, and attacks military targets in rural areas without minimizing the risk to the civilian population. All of these actions are violations of the most fundamental rules of international humanitarian law, or the laws of war, the most recent formulations of which are contained in the Geneva Conventions of 1949 and the Additional Protocols of 1977. In the period under review, Sendero not only has continued these practices but also has extended them to new regions within Peru. Because of Sendero's increased military activity, these violations have also increased in frequency. We are unaware of any initiative by the Sendero leadership to limit these abuses committed by guerrillas under its command. On the contrary, the leadership has publicly defended the practice of murdering those viewed as Sendero's political or class enemies.*

The other guerrilla group operating in Peru, the Movimiento Revolucionario Tupac Amaru (MRTA), also commits violations of the laws of war, particularly through the use of explosives in urban areas. However, after its spectacular incursion in the jungle region of San Martín in late 1987, the MRTA seems to have lost considerable strength, so the number of violations committed by its forces has decreased in 1988.

Americas Watch condemns these actions without reservation. For this purpose, we apply the standards set forth in Common Article 3 of the four Geneva Conventions of 1949, which explicitly address conflicts that are not of an international character. Protocol II of 1977 is a more complete and detailed instrument covering internal conflicts or civil wars, but in our view it does not apply to the current Peruvian situation because the insurgents do not exercise

---

* In defending a Sendero action in Lucanamarca in which his troops killed more than 80 peasants, Abimael Guzmán said: "There was an excuse there, as we analyzed in 1983, but everything in life has two sides: our problem was [to strike] a decisive blow to stop them, to make them understand that things were not so easy.... It was the Central Leadership itself that planned the action and decided things...." "President Gonzalo Rompe el Silencio," by Luis Arce Borja and Janet Talavera, El Diario, July 31, 1988, p. 19.

15

sufficient control over the population or territory to meet the demanding requirements for Protocol II to be applicable.* For its part, common Article 3 sets forth minimum rules which are easily understood and which, in our judgment, are applicable to the current Peruvian situation:

> "In the case of armed conflict not of an international character occurring in the territory of the High Contracting Parties, each Party to the conflict shall be bound to apply, as a minimum, the following provisions:

> (1) Persons taking no active part in the hostilities, including members of armed forces who have laid down their arms and those placed *hors de combat* by sickness, wounds, detention, or any other cause, shall in all circumstances be treated humanely, without any adverse distinction founded on race, color, religion or faith, sex, birth or wealth, or any other similar criteria.

> To this end, the following acts are and shall remain prohibited at any time and in any placed whatsoever with respect to the above-mentioned persons:

> (a) violence to life and person, in particular murder of all kinds, mutilation, cruel treatment and torture;

> (b) taking of hostages;

> (c) outrages upon personal dignity, in particular humiliating and degrading treatment;

> (d) the passing of sentences and the carrying out of executions without previous judgment pronounced by a regularly constituted court, affording all the judicial guarantees which are recognized as indispensable by civilized peoples.

> (2) The wounded and sick shall be collected and cared for.

---

*　Article 1 of Protocol II, entitled "Material field of application," reads as follows: "This Protocol, which develops and supplements Article 3 common to the Geneva Conventions of 12 August 1949 without modifying its existing conditions of application, shall apply to all armed conflicts which are not covered by Article 1 of the Protocol Additional to the Geneva Conventions of 12 August 1949, and relating to the Protection of Victims of International Armed Conflicts (Protocol I) and which take place in the territory of a High Contracting Party between its armed forces and dissident forces or other organized armed groups which, under responsible command, exercise such control over a part of its territory as to enable them to carry out sustained and concerted military operations and to implement this Protocol."

16

An impartial humanitarian body, such as the International-al Committee of the Red Cross, may offer its services to the Parties to the conflict.

The Parties to the conflict should further endeavor to bring into force, by means of special agreements, all of part of the other provisions of the present Convention

The application of the preceding provisions shall not affect the legal status of the Parties to the conflict."

It is worth pointing out that, in applying this standard, Americas Watch does not confer any special status on the insurgents, as the text itself makes clear. In addition, we note that the simple rules of behavior in combat that we apply are binding independently on each party without regard to the compliance of any other party, so that violations committed by one side are not excuse for those of another. Finally, these rules are to be respected and applied regardless of an insurgent group's political aim; international humanitarian law is neutral as to political objectives but places strict limits on the means employed.

In the course of our brief visit to Ayacucho, we had the occasion to visit the local hospital and interview two women who had been seriously wounded in an action by Sendero which violated these fundamental principles of the laws of war.

On July 3, 1988 Sendero Luminoso detonated a hand grenade at a dance in the city of Huamanga, capital of Ayacucho, apparently to protest the performance in the city of a popular musical group called "Los Shapis." More than thirty of those attending the dance were wounded, many of them seriously. In the hospital, we interviewed Albina Soto Quispe, a young mother of two, and her niece, Nélida Huayhua, as well as a relative who was taking care of them. Several days after the blast, both women had serious visible wounds caused by fragments of the grenade, although their lives were not in danger.

Sendero Luminoso did not claim credit for this attack; it usually makes no effort to confirm or deny its role in such actions. All the persons we consulted in Ayacucho, however, were certain that Sendero was responsible, particularly because "Los Shapis" had been threatened by Sendero on previous occasions. Those consulted by us discounted the possibility that the Army or police might have been responsible for the attack, both because these

17

government forces would not have had a motive for it, and because many soldiers and policemen attended the ball, although none of them was hurt. "Los Shapis" are extremely popular in Ayacucho and elsewhere, with their blend of Andean music and popular rhythms; in Ayacucho, however, sectors of the population who tend to sympathize with Sender resent what they perceive as manipulation of Andean culture by "Los Shapis."

The "Los Shapis" case is not unique in the difficulties it presents of determining whether a violation has been committed by Sendero or by other forces, including the Army or the police. On many occasions, perpetrators disguise themselves as their enemy, or leave misleading written or verbal statements in an attempt to incriminate that enemy. In the following examples of abuses committed by the insurgents between January and August 1988, we have deliberately left out cases in which evidence of the responsibility of Sendero or the MRTA was ambiguous. We have included only those examples in which the identity of the victims, the *modus operandi* of the attackers, or the presence of witnesses made it clear that the insurgents were responsible.*

Hugo Tello Mata, a United Left councilman in the city of Huanta, Ayacucho, was murdered by Sendero on July 21, 1988, on the road between Ayacucho and Huanta, as he drove a vehicle with passengers. Sendero blocked the road and accused Tello Mata of breaking the general strike in effect in all of Peru that day. He was shot and killed on the spot; the passengers were forced to walk barefoot to Huanta. (*Caretas,* July 25, 1988, p. 18)

Luciano Valderrama, an APRA (government party) leader and the lieutenant governor of Moyobamba, was murdered in January 1988 with two shots to the head. Sendero guerrillas broke into his house armed with a machine gun and revolvers, and shot him in the presence of his wife and children. The assailants left a note saying: "This is the way the APRA thieves and finks die."

Leocadio Mendoza Alarcón, a community leader in the settlement called "9 de Diciembre" in Ayacucho, and his wife, Antonia Padilla, were murdered in their home by a Sendero group, which left a note saying: "This is the way bribe-takers and swindlers die."

---

* Unless otherwise cited, these cases have been taken from <u>Reporte de Diarios y Revistas,</u> Jan.-Aug. 1988, a summary of items published in the Peruvian press, issued by the Centro de Estudios y Acción para la Paz (CEAPAZ), a Lima-based human rights organization. We have noted specific dates when they have been available.

A group of ten Senderistas intercepted a long-distance bus travelling between Huancayo and Ayacucho and checked the identity of the passengers. Manuel Medina Sobrino, a lieutenant in the Guardia Civil (police); his wife, Irene Alvarado Leyva; Wilfredo Palomino Canchipe, a sublieutenant in the Investigations Police (PIP); and Percy Aquije Nacahua, a PIP policeman, were taken out of the bus and forced to walk away from the road, where they were murdered.

Rodolfo Castro Mendoza, a police lieutenant and doctor, was killed by three shots to the head. He had been travelling from Huancayo to Ayacucho when his bus was intercepted by a Sendero group. After they identified him as a policeman, the Senderistas ordered him out of the bus and shot him on the spot.

In April 1988, three members of Sendero stopped a vehicle in Cuzco and killed Zózimo Huamán, the manager of the Tupac Amaru farming cooperative, and his wife, Juana Velázquez.

On March 25, 1988, a Sendero contingent invaded the village of Totora, Grau province, in Apurímac, and searched for the house of Santiago Chipana, the mayor. They killed Chipana with three gunshots.

Feliciano José Avila Castro, the lieutenant governor of Maynay, province of Huanta, Ayacucho, was shot to death by a Sendero contingent for "refusing to collaborate with armed struggle."

Sergio Canales Navarro, mayor of Huanta and a local APRA leader, was kidnapped from his home by a Sendero group. His corpse was found in a place called Cerro Blanco.

Isidoro García Vargas, an APRA leader and the mayor of Socabaya in Arequipa, was murdered in April 1988 by a Sendero group which also killed his driver, Jorge Supo Paucar.

Tito Alanya, an APRA activist, an engineer and the manager of a local office of the Development Corporation of Ayacucho (a government agency) in Huancasancos, was tied up inside his car by a Sendero squad; his assailants then blew up the vehicle with dynamite.

In San Juan de Salinas, Department of Puno, Sendero Luminoso shot and killed the mayor, Edilberto Jaime Centeno Jove, a member of the United Left coalition.*

---

* In addition, in our 1987 report we described the murder by Sendero of Zenobio Huarsaya, the mayor of San Juan de Salinas, who had preceded the above-noted Edilberto Jaime Centeno in that office. Huarsaya's murder, on April 8, 1987, came after a mock "popular trial" in which the community of San Juan de Salinas defended Huarsaya and pleaded unsuccessfully with Sendero to spare his life ("A Certain Passivity: Failure to Curb Human Rights Abuses in Peru," Americas Watch, New York, December 1987, p.20).

Two members of Sendero Luminoso shot and killed Luis Dueñas Peralta, mayor of the city of Puno, capital of the Department of Puno, in the Southern Andes. Dueñas was a prominent local leader of the government party, APRA.

In the province of Chihcha, south of Lima, Sendero killed another local APRA leader, Mario Ciro Casas Sánchez, a teacher and governor of the province. His assailants ambushed him when he was approaching his home and killed him with six gunshots.

Sendero Luminoso murdered two community leaders in Ticlayan, Cerro de Pasco: Humberto Salcedo Rodríguez, the president of the community's security committee, and Leonidias Gomez Yallico, a former trade union leader at the State-run mining company called CENTROMIN.

Two local leaders of the United Left coalition, Peru's largest opposition group, were killed by Sendero in the town of Progreso, Abancay. The victims, Andrés Trujillo Rodríguez, the mayor of Progreso, and Felipe Gutiérrez, a teacher, were accused by their killers of "electioneering" and being traitors.

As the preceding examples illustrate, the majority of Sendero's victims are democratically elected officials, community leaders and policemen who are killed after they surrender. International humanitarian law prohibits the killing or mistreatment of such people.

In addition, Sendero is said to have murdered sixty engineers and agricultural technicians since 1980. The apparent reason is Sendero's policy of opposing any and all development programs in the regions where they operate.* These attacks also violate international humanitarian law. Examples of such attacks during 1988 include the following:

At a drinking water development project in Coyllor, department of Junín, a Sendero contingent killed Gelegraldo Vilchez Zarate, 54, the assistant manager in charge of the Mántaro del Centro "micro-region," and his 22-year-old son, Fernando Vilchez.

In June, United States citizen Constantin Gregory, a 25-year-old agronomist from Los Angeles, was killed by Sendero in Sincos, province of Jauja, Junín Department, when his vehicle was stopped and he was identified as an official of the Agency for International Development (AID) working in a

---

* Si magazine, No. 80, September 5-12, 1988.

rural development project near Huancayo. The group also murdered Gregory's companion, Gustavo José Rojas Condorí, a 35-year-old Peruvian national employed in the same project. The project was designed to improve sheep and small farm animal production among local peasant communities.*

In addition, the MRTA has continued to commit serious violations. The MRTA claimed responsibility for two attacks against Carmen Rosa Cusquen Cabrera, a lawyer and the mother of a young boy. Cusquén's two brothers, apparently MRTA activists, had been killed previously. During the first attack in April, Cusquén was seriously wounded by survived. The second attack took placed in the Arzobispo Loayza Hospital in Lima, where she was being treated for those wounds. Cusquén died as a result of the second attack.

On July 2, 1988, the MRTA kidnapped 67-year-old retired Air Force General Héctor Jeri García, in an apparent attempt to obtain ransom. Two members of the MRTA, Miguel Pasache Vidal and Sócrates Porta Secano, entered into negotiations with his family over his release, and were arrested in their houses by persons identifying themselves as members of the PIP. After a few days, their corpses were found in the Lima neighborhoods of Cañete. On September 20, the Comando Rodrigo Franco, a new shadowy group described below, claimed credit for their execution. On October 23, 1988, General Jeri was released unharmed after his family, at the demand of the MRTA, distributed food in poor neighborhoods and published MRTA's statements in national magazines. In the previous two days, Mons. Augusto Beuzeville, the Auxiliary Catholic Bishop of Lima, had pleaded with the MRTA for the general's release.

---

*   "U.S. Agronomist Killed in Andes By Guerrillas," The Washington Post, June 16, 1988; "Maoist Rebels Slay a U.S. Agronomist and Peru Colleague," The New York Times, June 16, 1988.

V. THE LEGAL AND MILITARY ASPECTS OF THE GOVERNMENT'S COUNTER- INSURGENCY STRATEGY

A.   The State of Emergency

Article 231 of the Peruvian Constitution contemplates two forms of states of exception, or suspensions of constitutional guarantees, which may be invoked to address threats to peace and security. Since 1983, Peru has made extensive use of the milder of the two forms, called a "state of emergency,"* in certain areas, thereby restricting freedom of movement, freedom from unwarranted searches and seizures, freedom of association and freedom from arbitrary arrest.

During the current administration, a state of emergency has either been declared or retained in 36 provinces and two districts in a total of seven departments, including the department that encompasses Lima, the capital city. The following chart shows the number of Peruvians who currently live under such restrictions:**

Department	Population
Lima-Callao	4,608,010
Ayacucho	391,883
Huancavelica	346,797
San Martín	319,000
Apurímac	283,195
Pasco	160,483
Huánuco	137,493

---

*   The stricter form is called a "state of siege." For a more detailed explanation, see "A Certain Passivity," page 5, and García Sayán Diego, Peru: Estados de Excepción y Régimen Jurídico, in Comisión Andina de Juristas, Proceedings of a Seminar on States of Exception in the Andean Region, Lima, 1987.

**   Informe sobre Aplicación de Estado de Emergencia en el Perú, COMISEDH, Lima 1988.

Lima has been in a state of emergency since February 1986, and President Alan García has renewed that decision periodically. Lima had not been under a state of emergency during President Belaúnde's term. As the above chart shows, 36% of the population of Peru is affected by these restrictions. The areas under the state of emergency include Peru's three major geographic regions: the coast, the mountains and the jungle. In some of these areas, particularly in the jungle zones of Huánuco, Ayacucho, San Martin and even Pasco, there is extensive drug trafficking.

After more than six years of a state of emergency in various parts of the capital, there is little question that the imposition of a state of emergency can be legally justified by existing violence. Nonetheless, it is legitimate to ask whether invoking the state of emergency has been an effective tool, or whether, on the other hand, it has provided the legal framework for a proliferation of human rights violations. Our monitoring indicates that there is no direct relationship between the areas under a state of emergency and any reduction in the number or severity of terrorist acts or any increase in the success of the struggle against terrorism. On the contrary, a case can be made that in some places terrorist activity has actually increased once a state of emergency has been imposed. Unfortunately, the imposition of a state of emergency also has tended to correspond to an increase in human rights abuses.

The state of emergency restricts not only the insurgent groups, which tend in any event to be prepared to confront such constraints, but also the daily lives of the majority of the population, limiting the exercise of fundamental political rights. An important study conducted by Diego Garcia Sayan of the Andean Commission of Jurists provides several examples of the police broadly interpreting their powers under the state of emergency, at times by analogy to stated powers, in order to hold detainees for reasons unrelated to the insurgency for periods longer than those authorized by law.*

The most important feature of the Peruvian state of emergency is its provision for the appointment of a Politico-Military Command in each zone

---

* Diego García Sayán, "Habeas Corpus y Estados de Emergencia," Comisión Andina de Juristas, Lima, 1988.

where a state of emergency is declared. This Command, which effectively takes over the administration of the area, has been established in every zone except Lima. Lima has so far been exempted because the appointment of a Command there would mean that cabinet ministers and members of Congress would be subject to military authority, making a mockery of the constitutional regime.

The statute regulating the state of emergency is Law 24,150, promulgated in the last few weeks of President Belaúnde's term, apparently in response to demands from certain sectors in the Armed Forces. The statute grants extraordinary powers to the military chief in each emergency zone, a grant which has sparked considerable conflict between military and civilian authorities.* Although President García had promised to change President Belaúnde's counter-insurgency strategy, his government has made no effort to amend or repeal this law. In fact, the García administration cited Law 24,150 to justify granting the Armed Forces unencumbered powers to put down the prison riots in Lima and Callao in June 1986, producing the most tragic policy decision made by the García administration so far.

The establishment of a Politico-Military Command technically preserves the authority of the President and the Minister of Defense, who merely delegate their powers to the local military commander. In practice, and particularly in the perception of the population, elected leaders are deprived of authority and all effective power is vested in the military commanders — a perceived abdication of civilian responsibility.** The constitutionality of this clause is suspect, because while the state of emergency purportedly does not suspend

---

* The emergency powers are spelled out in Article 5 of the law, and they relate to public order and security. In practice, however, the chief of the Politico-Military Command exercises broader powers, such as restricting access to certain areas by the press or human rights monitors, as recently occurred to Juan Méndez of Americas Watch.

** The opinion that this represents an abdication of civilian authority was recently expressed in a report by the Special Congressional Commission on Causes of Violence and Peace Alternatives. The Commission unanimously recommended that the Senate submit to the Prime Minister a note expressing its willingness to negotiate a review of Law 24,150 as it relates to states of exception, with a view toward "returning to civilian authorities the political attributes of their responsibility." (p.12).

political rights, the law effectively deprives some officials of the right to exercise functions for which they have been elected.*

The role of the District Attorneys and the judiciary in the zones of emergency is technically unaffected by the imposition of a state of exception. Except in Lima, however, military restrictions do have an effect on the tasks performed by these institutions, particularly their role of protecting citizens' rights.

Although the Constitution explicitly requires the government to provide detailed reasons for establishing a state of emergency in a given zone, the government has not complied with this requirement. Nor has the government provided any information on the results achieved by the implementation of these emergency measures. The result is that the citizenry and the Congress have been denied the opportunity to evaluate and control these acts of government.

There are several bills pending in Congress to repeal Law 24,150 and to establish a system of civilian control over the zones being governed under a state of emergency. One such bill, submitted by Senator César Delgado, now the Minister of Justice, would give Cabinet-level rank to the official appointed to implement the state of emergency in a given region. These and other proposals would contribute to the re-establishment of clear democratic authority in the conflict zones. Unfortunately, these bills are not being actively discussed in Congress.

B.   Anti-Terrorist Legislation

In his address to Congress of July 28, 1988, President Alan García announced that the Executive would propose sweeping amendments to the existing anti-terrorist legislation. Several bills were submitted in the next few days, and at the time of this writing they are being discussed in the pertinent committees. The President proposes to repeal Law 24,700, enacted only in 1987, which

---

*   Several Peruvian jurists have expressed the view that the powers granted by Law 24,150 to the Politico-Military Commands are unconstitutional. See, e.g., Enrique Bernales and Marcial Rubio, Constitución: Fuentes e Interpretación, Mesa Redonda, Lima, 1988, p. 108.

establishes the procedures for the investigation and trial of crimes of terrorism. He also proposes to redefine the offense of terrorism and to increase its penalty; to create new offenses such as "terrorist association" (a special form of conspiracy) and public advocacy of terrorism (*apología*); and to eliminate judicial leniency or remission of penalty through repentance or cooperation for terrorist-related crimes.

This effort to amend current law arises out of a series of perceived inadequacies that do not always withstand scrutiny. The statute that currently criminalizes acts of terrorism is Law 24,651, in effect since March 1987. This Act repealed and replaced the previous anti-terrorist law, Legislative Decree 46, which had been enacted during President Belaúnde's term. The law that currently sets forth the procedures for investigating, prosecuting and trying crimes committed with a terrorist purpose is Law 24,700, enacted by Congress in June 1987.

Law 24,651 is very similar to a statute in effect in Spain which was designed to address terrorist crimes. The Peruvian law does not criminalize membership in a terrorist association (conspiracy) or the advocacy of terrorism (apología), as Decree 46, its predecessor, had done. In addition, following modern developments in criminal law in Italy and Spain, and responding to suggestions made by certain experts and independent publications, Law 24,651 introduced clauses providing for leniency or exemption from punishment for those who, having committed terrorist acts, repented or collaborated with the investigation and prosecution.

The law has been criticized for employing terminology that is too vague.* The text also contains some internal inconsistencies which have made

---

*   Article 288A, for example, proscribes "acts that might create danger" or are "meant to cause the destruction or deterioration of [property]...."

it difficult to apply.* There has been no evaluation, however, of why this statutory formula has failed. In our view, the cause is not only the technical defects but also a lack of political will on the part of the government to promote the use of prosecutorial discretion in the fashion contemplated by the drafters of the statute.

The procedural law for the trial of these cases, Law 24,700, introduced a number of safeguards for detainees during the investigative stage, in line with the principle that every defendant is innocent until proven guilty. Such safeguards included the requirements that the police give immediate notice to the prosecutor upon arresting a suspect, that the right to counsel not be subject to waiver, that only a judge can place a person in incommunicado detention, that detainees be given routine medical examinations, and that human rights organizations be permitted to act in the defense of detainees at an early stage.

For example, Article 2 of Law 24,700 established that prosecutors are in charge of investigations:

> "The fiscal provincial [district attorney] will be directly in charge of the investigation, in order to defend legality, human rights and the interests protected by law. Members of the police forces participate and act in the investigative measures ordered by the fiscal."

This aspect of the statute has been severely criticized by law enforcement and government officials and by some media, on the ground that the new role given to the prosecutor hampered investigations into acts of terrorism. Even though

---

* In copying the Spanish statute, the Peruvian law incurred a grammatical error. The Spanish law allows for total cancellation of the penalty when the active collaboration of the defendant has been instrumental in identifying criminals, impeding the commission of crime, or hampering the development of terrorist gangs, as long as the defendant himself is not charged with being the author of actions that have caused death or injuries to others. The Peruvian version substituted "sancionado" (a convicted defendant) where the Spanish law read "imputado" (an accused defendant). The result was to make it impossible to apply this principle, because it could only be applied after a defendant had already been convicted. By then, his repentance is meaningless for the investigation; the prospect of remaining in prison until the end of a long trial does not give the defendant the incentive to cooperate that is the secret of the success of the European experiment. See La Red (Bulletin of the School of Human Rights), No. 20-21, June 1988, Instituto de Defensa Legal, Lima.

this clause merely applied in the terrorism context a more general statute that has been in effect since 1981,* General Fernando Reyes Roca, currently the Director of PIP and formerly Chief of DIRCOTE, has said that the new law made police work very difficult because, unlike police officers, prosecutors have no training or experience in conducting investigations.

In another important addition, Law 24,700 established a mandatory role for defense counsel in all steps of the investigation (instrucción). Article 2 states:

> "The participation of counsel is indispensable in every one of the actions taken. The right to counsel cannot be waived. If for any reason the defense lawyer fails to appear at two consecutive citations, the State's attorney must immediately appoint another lawyer for the defense."

These and other guarantees enshrined in Law 24,700 were intended to provide effective protection for the defendant to exercise his rights as provided in the Constitution and in international instruments to which Peru is a party, such as the American Convention of Human Rights. In the context described in this report, in which disappearances, extrajudicial executions and torture are common occurrences, this law was understood as an important means of protection.**

A significant shortcoming of the law is that it extends its added due process protections only to persons under investigation for crimes of terrorism; other detainees under investigation for common crimes enjoy considerably

---

*   Ley Orgánica del Ministerio Público (Legislative Decree 52, enacted April 3, 1981), the law that organizes and regulates the office of the prosecutor, provides in Article 9:
"In accordance with Article 250, sec. 5 of the Constitution, the Office of the Prosecutor oversees and intervenes in the investigation of crime starting at the police stage. For that purpose, the police forces conduct the investigation. The Office of the Prosecutor takes part in it, providing guidance as to the evidence that needs to be gathered, and oversees it to ensure compliance with legal norms for the timely exercise of penal action."

**   According to a poll conducted by Instituto de Defensa Legal in 1984, which interviewed defendants accused of terrorism who claimed not to be members of any armed organization, 91.7% had suffered mistreatment at the initial stages of the investigation, 96.42% had no lawyer at the time of their first interrogation, and 98.2% had not been offered a free, court-appointed lawyer, as Peruvian law requires.

diminished guarantees. In our view, discriminatory treatment is unreasonableand should be corrected, not by abolishing the new safeguards, but by making them available to all defendants. Peruvian human rights organizations, which seek to protect all individuals who may be subject to mistreatment or injustice, have presented a draft bill to the Executive Branch along these lines which has not been accepted.*

With regard to the role assigned to public prosecutors at the early stages of a criminal investigation — a role that prosecutors successfully play in many countries — it is clear that Peruvian prosecutors are ill-prepared to assume that function. But that weakness in the law can and should be corrected by adequate training and qualification of prospective and acting prosecutors. The alternative — eliminating this prosecutorial role altogether — returns the conduct of investigations to the police, who are only marginally better prepared for it; meanwhile, the prosecutors' important role in protecting human rights and supervising investigative operations is abandoned. There is ample evidence in Peru to show that, when such controls are lifted, a pattern of serious human rights violations emerges.

In any event, the legitimate critique of some aspects of this legislation cannot possibly justify, as President García now proposes, the repeal of the entire law, including the elimination of its provisions barring waiver of the right to counsel, requiring immediate notice to the prosecutor of an arrest, authorizing only judges to impose *incommunicado* detention, providing for mandatory and routine medical examination of detainees, and allowing human rights organizations to act in the defense of a detainee at an early stage. These protections are not meant to undermine the work of the police and in due course they should not; instead, their proper enforcement should contribute to the professionalization of police work. The repeal of these rules, because it would signal a retreat from a clear commitment to the protection of human rights in the course of

---

*   Proyecto de Ley sobre los Derechos del Detenido, IDL, Lima, July 1987. This is a proposed bill, introduced before the National Council of Human Rights by Carlos Chipoco Cáceda, the representative of human rights organizations at that governmental body. It represents an attempt by the human rights community to propose legal alternatives to prevent and eliminate the practice of torture, mistreatment and disappearances.

criminal investigations, is likely to give the green light to severe human rights violations.

The substantive portions of the bills introduced by the Executive also deserve close scrutiny. For example, the new description of offenses is overbroad and imprecise, such as defining a terrorist act as an act committed with the purpose of altering the democratic system as established in the Constitution, destabilizing the constitutional government, or *affecting the security of the state*" (emphasis added). The lack of a precise definition of "security of the state" would give police and military forces, as well as judges, unduly great latitude in enforcing this law.*

Human rights organizations have been critical of the government's proposed statutory amendments. For example, the Lima-based *Instituto de Defensa Legal* (IDL) has said:

> "[The proposed amendments] eliminate the purpose of generating fear [from the definition of the crime of terrorism], which is, precisely, a specific feature of the terrorist *modus operandi*. Instead, subjective elements are included which are terribly ambiguous and deeply ideological: '...purpose of altering the democratic order established in the Constitution, destabilizing the constitutional government or affecting the security of the state...'; a new perception of this crime emerges: terrorism becomes a crime against the State. In other words, terrorist behavior is equivalent to subversive behavior." (Victor Prado and Miguel Talavera, *Proyecto Sustitutorio de la Sección Octava A del Código Penal*, IDL, Lima, 1988).

In addition, as the proposed law recognizes, there is a need for legislation establishing the crime of "terrorist association," which is not currently encompassed by the Criminal Code (since the repeal of Decree 46). This need arises in light of the clandestine form of organization and the collective action of the insurgent groups. Likewise, the mere possession of explosives or

---

* This violates a fundamental principle of criminal law, known in many countries as the "principle of legality." In the Peruvian Constitution, it is established as follows: "Nobody shall be prosecuted or convicted for acts or omissions which, at the time they were committed, had not been previously qualified in the law, in an express and unequivocal manner, as a sanctionable offense, nor punished with a penalty not contemplated in the law." (Article 2, Sec.20, paragraph "D," emphasis added).

31

unauthorized weapons is currently sanctioned only by confiscation — a glaring omission which the proposed law would correct.

We are concerned, however, at the inclusion in the proposed law of the offense of "advocacy" (*apología* or *elogio*) of terrorism, because of its potential effect on freedom of expression. Our concern arises in part, again, from the imprecision and breadth of the text, which would punish even the person who publicly extolls the virtues of "developments having to do with terrorists or with terrorist acts." This is so broad that it might lead to the prosecution of a journalist who writes a report which — in the opinion of the police or a judge — refers favorably to acts of terrorism. Because there is no connection or relationship required between the terrorist act and the expression of support, the law sweeps too widely and leaves an unacceptably broad margin of discretion to the enforcer. It is extremely difficult to define the limits of *apologia* under any circumstance; in the case of Peru, it is all the more difficult because of the broad and expansive manner in which law enforcement bodies have interpreted their powers.In the view of Americas Watch, the inclusion of a criminal offense like *apología del crimen* constitutes an illegitimate restriction of press freedom and freedom of thought, as established in the international instruments signed and ratified by Peru.

By contrast, Americas Watch believes that it is appropriate to criminalize the act of instigating a crime. In this regard, we note that the Criminal Code of Peru already contemplates this form of criminal responsibility* and that there is no obstacle to applying such a provision to those cases in which the instigation emboldens someone else to commit a terrorist crime.

Finally, we are in full agreement with the need to criminalize the illegal or unauthorized possession of firearms. The violence that pervades Peru has many roots, but it is undoubtedly fueled by the easy availability of firearms. We support the government's initiative to limit the calibres and types of weapons

---

*   Article 100 provides: "Whoever takes part in the execution of an act, or intentionally causes some one else to commit it, or willfully provides support or cooperation without which the act could not be performed, shall be punished with the same sanction as the author of the actionable offense."

that can be legally put in civilian hands, and to establish severe penalties for breaches of this regulation.

C. Administration of Justice

In the period under study, the failures of Peru's system of justice have again been a major contributing factor to the denial of basic rights. The judiciary is hardly independent of the Executive Branch, it is woefully under-financed, and its members lack adequate professional and academic training. For these reasons, the Judicial Branch fails in its responsibility to protect citizens and to provide inexpensive and swift justice for their claims. The public perceives that judges are not trustworthy; that impunity for major crimes is rampant; that, on the other hand, an innocent citizen may well be victimized by judicial error; and that it is difficult, costly and time-consuming even to try to seek redress. Most Peruvians also think that the judicial system is thoroughly corrupt, and that money and influence-peddling is tolerated in most quarters as a means for resolving disputes or accelerating judicial outcomes. Many narcotics offenders, for example, have been able to buy their way out of judicial trouble. A Peruvian jurist has stated that:

> "[The Judicial Branch] has made institutional efforts to address this problem; reality shows, however, that they are insufficient while obsolete procedures remain in place that are an invitation to corruption, and while the judiciary retains inadequate mechanisms to recruit judges and officers, as well as apects of judicial organization that foster irregularities."[*]

Two cases illustrate the paradoxical results that the Peruvian system of justice can yield:

> In June 1988, police forces captured Osmán Morote Barrionuevo, one of Sendero Luminoso's most important leaders (he is supposed to be the top military commander in the organization). He was captured with abundant written information about the group, including plans for future operations. His arrest, hailed as a major police victory, seems to

---

[*] Javier de Belaúnde, "Rescatando la Justicia," Caretas, July 25, 1988. About the undemocratic aspects of Peruvian justice, see: Luis Pasara, "Perú: Administración de Justicia?," in La Administración de Justicia en América Latina, Consejo Latinoamericano de Derecho y Desarrollo, Lima, 1984.

have been the result of good intelligence work and a substantial dose of luck on the part of the police, combined with carelessness on Sendero's part. The arrest seems to have had a significant impact on Sendero. In late July, *El Diario* published a long, exclusive interview with Abimael Guzmán, Sendero's leader. Many analysts speculate that the interview was an attempt by Guzmán to confront a state of disarray throughout the ranks as a result of Morote's arrest. Morote was held at DIRCOTE headquarters and later in the Canto Grande prison. He faces charges before several different courts. He came to trial on the first charge in July, amid great public attention and media coverage, and was acquitted. Although legal experts viewed the acquittal more as the result of shoddy evidence gathering than of inadequate laws,* the acquittal provoked another round of calls for legislative reform, particularly demands to criminalize "terrorist association" (conspiracy) as a separate crime. Morote remains in prison awaiting trial on the several other charges he faces. And on October 19, the Twelfth Criminal Court of Lima convicted Morote of terrorism, for his role in attacks in Lima and its suburbs beginning in 1981, and sentenced him to a 15-year prison term. Morote has appealed the conviction and sentence to the Supreme Court.

Morote's acquittal in the first case generated intense debate in the media and political circles about the weakness of judges and current laws. Few used the occasion to insist that the police should do better police work. Admiral Juan Soria, the Minister of Interior, has stated that 95% of those accused of terrorism and brought before the courts are released.** Although these figures may be exaggerated, they reveal the incapability of Peru's legal system effectively to repress crime. Leniency or ineffectiveness on the part of judges — which, of course, works in favor of non-security offenders as well — is not the only cause, however: police bodies who are content with obtaining a "confession" as the sole evidence for the prosecution must share the blame. If the system thus results in unacceptable permissiveness for law-breakers, it also generates great injustice for innocent people.

---

* For the most part, the evidence submitted by police in support of prosecution consists of extra-judicial confessions that are later recanted before a judge. Those confessions are often obtained by force or, at the very least, without the assistance of counsel. Even when they are nominally made before a prosecutor, the latter frequently only signs the statement after the fact.

** Interview with Caretas, July 25, 1988.

34

In the second case, Francisco Landeo Jurado was arrested by the PIP in Cuzco on March 24, 1983. Originally from Huancavelica, Landeo worked in a modest keyshop and supported his wife and three young children. Upon his arrest, he spent the first 40 days at the Cuzco police station. The reason for his arrest was an outstanding warrant issued by a court in Lima; after the first 40 days he was transferred to the capital. Between 1983 and 1986 he was able to see the judge on only three occasions, the first to give his initial statement and the other two to be confronted with witnesses he had never seen before. The file then was lost, and only in 1987 did his wife manage to locate it at a court in Cuzco. Landeo repeatedly requested his transfer to Cuzco to speed up the trial, but his requests were not granted. The court in Cuzco, meanwhile, decided to place the file "in reserve" awaiting Landeo's capture, even though Landeo by then had spent four years in custody without being convicted of any crime. The case has now been taken up by the *Comisión Episcopal de Acción Social* (CEAS), whose lawyers have filed an application for *amparo* based on the prolonged delay of justice. Landeo has publicly condemned Sendero Luminoso.*

These two cases are extreme, but by no means isolated, examples of the failures of the Peruvian judicial system, trapped as it is between a lack of resources and its own incapacity to change. The problem is of staggering proportions, but its solution is vital to the future of human rights in Peru. For that reason, the authorities must address the need for judicial reform promptly and vigorously. Structural change must be introduced to speed up the judicial process, to ensure the effective assistance of counsel, to equip officials with better technical and legal training, and to ensure some type of accountability for those responsible for administering the system of justice.

D.   The Military's Counter-Insurgency Strategy

The *Instituto de Defensa Legal* (IDL) has conducted a study of the current counter-insurgency strategy by analyzing anti-subversive manuals prepared by the Armed Forces in light of IDL's own experience in representing prisoners of conscience.** Some officers consulted by IDL have stated that the anti--

---

*   See his interview by Mariella Balvi in La República, May 30, 1988.

**   The study is part of a broader research program on peace alternatives conducted jointly by IDL, the Comisión Andina de Juristas (CAJ) and the Instituto Socialismo y Democracia.

subversive manuals are not now followed because the conditions of the current struggle against Sendero and MRTA are very different from those addressed by the manuals. Nonetheless, review of the manuals is important because they set forth the theoretical framework that was used to train the higher-ranking officers (colonels and generals) who are conducting the war today.

These manuals were written after the experience of fighting the short-lived guerrilla groups of the 1960s. Reflecting a "cold war" perspective, they explain the subversive phenomenon as the result of a bi-polar world, reduced to its East-West dimension. This strong ideological content helps explain why individuals are often targeted for arrest or trial as subversives — not on the basis of particular acts they may have committed, but because they harbor ideas that are deemed incompatible with Western thought. Like the doctrine of national security that has been applied in Argentina and other countries since the 1960s, the manuals' definition of "subversive" is not limited to the armed enemy combatant, but extends to anyone who questions the existing social order.

These manuals suggest the possibility of arresting innocent people on the ground that "they have information and their statements can lead to the arrest of insurgent leaders." The manuals also urge the "elimination" of members of the so-called "political-administrative organization" (as the enemy group is called) in the swiftest and most effective way possible — a clear allusion to the extra-legal killings that in fact have been committed repeatedly in the emergency zone.

This conception of the war includes no reference to the rights and interests of the civilian population. As a result, the Armed Forces in the emergency zone behave like an occupation army. Almost all soldiers operating in these highland and jungle areas come from Peru's coastal plains, and the officers seldom speak the local quechua language. This cultural and linguistic distance exacerbates the hostility and racial prejudice that exists between many Peruvians from the coast and those from the Andes.

According to the manuals, the war against subversion is "irregular," "permanent" and "total." "Irregular" means that there is no confrontation between clearly identified camps, wearing uniforms and defending specific territory. The consequence is that the rules of war established in the Geneva

36

Conventions are deemed not to apply.* The "permanent" nature of war means that, as opposed to conventional war, the fighting is not viewed as limited to the opposition's use of firearms, but is considered to include, for example, opposition efforts to organize a general strike. The war is said to be "total" because it is fought on not only military but also economic, social, psychological and other fronts. In this conception, paradoxical as it may sound, there is room for those who favor systematic abuse of international humanitarian law, and at the same time have a genuine concern for economic and social policy as part of an overall counterinsurgency strategy.

The frailness of Peruvian democracy also weakens the motivation of the government soldiers who are charged with carrying out the fight. While *senderistas* and *tupacamaristas* are imbued with a sense of political purpose, most military and police officers see their fighting as a professional duty, and troops generally fight only because they are forced to. The military leadership

---

* Some conservative military leaders even propose that the laws of war do not apply to conventional warfare, echoing similar statements by their Argentine colleagues. Brigadier General Gastón Ibáñez O'Brien has said:

"Gentlemen, there is no clean war; clean war died with the roving knights; all wars are dirty. What happens is that the dirt comes to light only in regards to the losers, not the winners. In the last World War, for example, had the Allies lost, Truman and the whole political and military leadership would surely have been tried as war criminals for throwing two atomic bombs. And those who exterminated the Jews would have been heroes. It is unreal to think that war is clean and that it will be conducted in the battlefield, armed with a lance. Violations, outrages, torture and all kinds of abuse have existed and will continue to exist for as long as there is war, because human passion is impossible to contain, and because no command can control all of its component forces, since there are circumstances in which an individual acts alone and must make decisions. Of course, no one approves of this, but we must recognize that it is part of the war phenomenon."

Speech transcribed in <u>Democracia y Violencia en el Perú</u>, Diego García, Sayan, ed., CEPEI, Lima, 1988, pg.108. This statement brings to mind a similar remark to the press made by General Roberto Viola, then President-designate of Argentina, in Washington in 1981, to the effect that if the Axis had won the war, the Nuremberg trials would have been held in Virginia. The ideas of Viola and Ibáñez run counter not only to the widely accepted understanding of the scope of humanitarian law but also to historic precedent: there are wars in which the contenders have by and large respected international humanitarian law, such as the Falklands-Malvinas conflict of 1982. In the case of Peru, Ibáñez's speech also breaks with the honorable tradition of naval hero Miguel Grau, renowned for his respect and consideration for enemies who had surrendered or whose lives were in danger.

in the emergency zone has attempted to compensate for this lack of psychological motivation with sheer and often misguided aggressiveness, in turn generating fear and mistrust among the population.

We believe that the democratic government of Peru must change the theory under which it conducts its war, and replace it with one that affirms the values of democracy: protection of human life, freedom of thought, and respect for the rights of persons. The government must also develop educational programs in human rights for its officer corps and troops, particularly among those charged with fighting the insurgents or with seeking them out among the population, identifying them and arresting them.

VI. HUMAN RIGHTS VIOLATIONS IN 1987 AND 1988

A.   Disappearances

From the beginning of the war unleashed by Sendero Luminoso, Peru has been plagued by the phenomenon of disappearances which has haunted Latin America since the 1960's. The practice in Peru is generally limited to the region of Ayacucho, which is Sendero's most important battleground and the locale of its greatest civilian support. The practice has been applied more selectively than in other countries, so the number of victims has not reached the tragic figures of Guatemala, El Salvador or the years of the "dirty war" in Argentina.

At the same time, it is worth noting, as we have before, that under President Alan García there has been a noticeable reduction in the number of disappearances in comparison to Fernando Belaúnde's presidency.* Several factors are to be credited with this partial success in the struggle against disappearances, including the work of domestic human rights organizations to sensitize public opinion, and the action of public officials who are not under the authority of the Executive Branch. The principal factor, however, has been the determination of the President and his government to rein in security forces.

Despite this reduction in frequency, disappearances continue, of both the temporary and permanent variety. Our use of the term "temporary disappearance" refers to a pattern whereby a person is located only after insistent requests by relatives, judges or prosecutors, and then only after several days or

---

* Between the establishment of the state of emergency in Ayacucho (December 1982) and President García's inauguration (July 1985) there were about 1,500 unresolved disappearances, or about 600 cases a year. Between July 1985 and December 1987 (a similar two-and-a-half-year period), unresolved disappearances totaled 250, or an average of 100 per year. The percentage of "re-appearances," i.e., disappeared detainees who are later found, is much higher under President García than under President Belaúnde: 50% of all disappearance cases are now favorably resolved, whereas in the early years very few of the disappeared were ever found.

weeks of unacknowledged detention, forced isolation and irregular *incommunicado* detention. The existence of a pattern of such cases — as well as of those in which the person is never found — and the failure of the authorities to investigate or punish a single such case, indicates to us that disappearances are still a deliberate policy of the armed and security forces in the emergency zone.

A report made on the basis of complaints filed with the prosecutor's office* reveals that in 1987 prosecutors received complaints about 122 persons who had disappeared, 46 of whom were eventually released or transferred to the PIP for appropriate prosecution; seven were found dead, their corpses in clandestine burial sites. The remaining 69, including 7 women and 9 minors, are still listed as "disappeared."

In another study conducted by APRODEH using data supplied by the *Coordinadora Nacional de Derechos Humanos*, a sample of 1137 complaints filed between January 1983 and March 1988 was fed into a computer. The study revealed that 785 of the victims were still disappeared, 169 had been located, and in 183 cases there was no confirmation of the original complaint.** Most of the unconfirmed cases are from 1983 and 1984; on the other hand, the great majority of the "reappeared" are from 1987 (127) and early 1988 (34). For the first time in 1987, there were more reappearances than permanent disappearances (127 against 114), although that trend was partially reversed in the first part of 1988 (34 against 48). Classified by the occupation of the victim, the disappeared were made up of 51% peasants, 23% students and 12% teachers. In 817 of the 1137 cases it had been possible to identify the agents responsible for the original arrest: in 58% of the cases, the Army was responsible, while 12.5% of

---

* "Las Desapariciones en el Perú durante 1987," Comisión de Derechos Humanos (COM-ISEDH), Lima, March 1988.

** The figure of 1137 constitutes a large sample; the total number of complaints received by the Prosecutor's Office is close to 2,500, of which more than 1,800 are considered "permanent disappearances." The APRODEH study reports 246 complaints in 1987, double those reported by the Prosecutor's Office for the same period, according to COMISEDH. The discrepancy reflects the fact that many disappearances are not reported to the Prosecutor.

40

the arrests were traced to the Civil Guard, a police body.* This record leaves Peru with the dubious distinction of being among the countries in Latin America, and indeed the world, with the largest number of reported disappearances.**

As the preceding paragraphs show, President Alan García's initiatives in this area deserve full support, but they clearly have not been sufficient to put an end to the practice. As the President has entered the second half of his five-year term, initial hopes that the reduction of the first few months would signal an end to disappearances have vanished. Moreover, there has been no serious investigation into any of the past or more recent disappearance cases. Only one case has reached the civilian courts: the disappearance of journalist Jaime Ayala Sulca in Huanta in 1984, which is blamed on Navy Captain Alvaro Artaza Adrianzén (aka "Camión"). When the case was about to come to trial, Artaza was the victim of a clearly faked kidnapping. Months later, Artaza filed petitions with the court without revealing his whereabouts, and the Tribunal of Constitutional Guarantees, incredibly, ruled in his favor, so that the case against him is now dead. The Navy cooperated in this travesty by publicly reporting Artaza's alleged kidnapping and by feeding other false information to the press. As its complicity came to light, the Navy retreated into a defiant silence.

It is clear, therefore, that the agents of disappearances are still certain that they will not be investigated and will not have to answer for their actions, either in criminal courts or before administrative tribunals. This impunity helps maintain, and even increase, the unacceptably high level of disappearances despite the President's actions.

In the last few months, human rights organizations have noted an increase in the number of new disappearance complaints, as well as an increase

---

*   A similar study was done by the Comisión de Estudios y Acción para la Paz (CEAPAZ) on the basis of 646 cases on which the Legal Department of CEAS had worked. The results closely paralleled those of the APRODEH study. Cómputo, CEAPAZ, Lima, April 1988

** See the most recent Report by the United Nations Working Group on Disappearances. In 1987, the Working Group received the most new complaints of disappearances, 79, from Peru; second place went to Guatemala, with 50. Document Number: E/CN.4/1988/19.

in the percentage of unresolved cases. In June 1988 alone, the Ayacucho office of the Prosecutor received 47 complaints, several of them with multiple victims; the number of reported disappeared persons was between 70 and 80. Most of these cases were in the area of Huanta, with the remainder in the provinces of La Mar and Cangallo; all of these areas are considered "red" (i.e. pro-Sendero) by the Army.* As explained elsewhere in this report, General José Valdivia, Chief of the Politico-Military Command of Ayacucho, prevented an Americas Watch monitor from visiting Huanta. Nonetheless, reliable sources in that city, consulted by other human rights organizations, confirm that the number of disappearances in the surroundings of Huanta between June and early July 1988 exceeded 80 victims.

In our visit to Huamanga, we obtained direct confirmation of a recent disappearance case which is clearly attributable to the Army:

> On June 29, 1988, uniformed Army troops kidnapped Guzmán Bautista Palomino, Gregorio Ipurre Ramos, Humberto Ipurre, Benigna Palomino de Ipurre and Catalina Ramos Palomino, all from their homes in Cayara. The first two were witnesses to the Cayara massacre of May 14, 1988, described at greater length later in this report, and the other three are the parents and sister of Ipurre. Guzmán Bautista Palomino had spoken to congressional investigators and to *Caretas* journalists about the events. When the Prosecutor came to Cayara, a military officer tried to bribe Bautista not to testify; the witness declined the money but still refused to testify out of fear of reprisal. On the other hand, Ipurre was one of the Prosecutor's key witnesses to the May events, and he had talked to all of the investigative delegations that had visited the village. According to the victims' relatives, interviewed by Americas Watch, the men in uniform broke into the different houses at night, beat both witnesses to the original massacre and, despite the protests of wives and children, took them away to the Army base, not more than two blocks away.

> The wives and children followed the captors to the base, but were threatened and had to leave. Hours later, other neighbors saw the detainees as they were being placed in trucks which left in the direction of another base in Huancapi. Despite formal complaints and informal inquiries by relatives, none of the detainees have reappeared.

---

*   Interview with the Ayacucho Prosecutor-Commissioner for Disappearances, Carlos Escobar Pineda, Huamanga, Ayacucho, July 8, 1988.

In an attempt to sow confusion, a few hours before the kidnapping unknown persons entered Cayara and placed flags and signs attributed to Sendero. In addition, a few days after the event, the Lima daily *El Comercio* published a report saying that unspecified "authorities" of Cayara accused Sendero of this kidnapping.* It is simply unthinkable, however, that Sendero could have operated, in Army uniform, in several houses, all a few yards away from a base that is 20 men strong. Besides, eyewitnesses saw the victims as they were taken away precisely to that base, and then forced to board military vehicles. All of this, plus the evident motive of obstructing the investigation, points to the Army as the clear culprit.

On July 11, 1988, Americas Watch wrote an urgent letter to President Alan García (see appendix) asking for guarantees for the reappearance, alive, of the witnesses to the Cayara massacre and their relatives. We have received no response to date.

On the basis of this data, Americas Watch fears that the practice of disappearances in the emergency zone is once again beginning to gather momentum, despite efforts to check it by civilian authorities in Huamanga, Special Prosecutor Carlos Escobar, and relatives of victims and human rights organizations. Preliminary data also suggest that in San Martín there have been cases of disappearances related to the inception of rural guerrilla operations by Sendero and MRTA in certain jungle areas of that Department. About 60 complaints have been filed by individuals or organizations based in the region. The Chief Prosecutor (*Fiscal de la Nación*) briefly commissioned Dr. Escobar to act as special commissioner for the same purpose in San Martín, and Escobar was apparently able to locate more than half of the cases reported. But without a decisive attitude on the part of the central government, and without specific actions to send the unmistakable signal that such practices are not tolerated, the heroic and risky efforts of these officials and institutions will be insufficient to put a stop to abuses by security agents who act under promise of impunity, and disappearances will continue to haunt Peru.

---

* "Patrulla militar dió muerte a seis subversivos en enfrentamiento," El Comercio, July 17, 1988.

B.   Torture

The use of torture and other forms of cruel, inhuman or degrading treatment, forbidden by Peru's international obligations as well as by domestic law, is nonetheless the method habitually used by police bodies to interrogate those suspected of both common and security offenses. We know of no governmental initiative to curb this practice. Judicial and prosecutorial officials throughout the country coexist with torture and do little or nothing to eliminate it, even though the Criminal Code makes torture a criminal offense.

As in most Latin American countries, a confession is given full evidentiary weight only when it is rendered before a judge. Nonetheless, a defendant's extra-judicial statements, even though recanted later, can be used against him as indicia or circumstantial evidence of guilt, whether or not the evidence establishes that it was obtained under torture. That this evidence is not automatically null and void undoubtedly contributes to the pervasive use of torture by interrogators. An even more important factor, however, is the lack of political will to end torture by enforcing the laws that proscribe it. As in other areas, impunity helps perpetuate the practice.

Americas Watch has talked recently with social and religious workers who visit prisons regularly to provide services to inmates. They told us that practically all inmates say they have been tortured while in the custody of PIP or DIRCOTE. The rare exceptions are women in advanced stages of pregnancy.

Torture is also regularly used against the disappeared. The methods in these cases are even more cruel and ferocious, since the object of the disappearance is precisely to avoid outside scrutiny of the interrogation and to maintain the impunity of the interrogators. Survivors of temporary disappearances have said that they were subjected to torture in military or police quarters, generally in the course of interrogation.

In DIRCOTE and PIP, according to sources who have interviewed a large number of detainees, the methods are brutal but primitive: beatings are pervasive, as are mock executions, threats with firearms, the "submarine" (forcing the prisoner's head into water almost to the point of drowning), and hanging prisoners from their wrists for hours. In the clandestine detention centers

44

were the disappeared are held, the captors use all of these methods as well as more sophisticated ones, such as the electric prod.

The Minister of Interior and the high police chiefs interviewed by Americas Watch denied that forces under their command use torture as an investigative technique. On the other hand, they complained that a large number of DIRCOTE officers are implicated in criminal complaints of torture; an official told us that 30% of DIRCOTE officers have had to answer charges of that nature. None of these officers has been removed from his position, even temporarily to facilitate the inquiry, and no one has been punished. The Minister and police chiefs attribute the large number of complaints exclusively to what they see as a deliberate strategy by "the subversives," advised by their lawyers, to complain of torture at the first possible opportunity in order to nullify evidence against them.

This rigid refusal to concede any illicit conduct by interrogators reflects, in our view, not excessive confidence in their subordinates, but an attempt to deny the undeniable. The willingness to close one's eyes to reality bodes poorly for the future because if officials who are in a position to investigate and punish abuses refuse even to consider that those abuses take place, the outcome will necessarily be continued impunity.

Law 24,700, enacted in 1987 and described above, did not help stem the use of torture. The duty of prosecutors to be present during every investigative step has been observed only nominally. *Fiscales* either are not prepared to confront the police, or see themselves as a part of law enforcement bodies, or simply choose not to get involved. Often the prosecutors simply sign documents prepared by the police without having been present during the act described.

Although Law 24,700 has not been adequately enforced, police forces have openly complained that it ties their hands and hampers the effectiveness of the struggle against terrorism. The government has taken the same position and, as noted above, has submitted to Congress a bill to repeal Law 24,700. No matter what legislation eventually replaces Law 24,700, any repeal that does not vindicate the positive aspects of the law in attempting to defend the fundamental right to the physical integrity of the person can only result in an increase in abuse on the part of DIRCOTE interrogators.

There has been another serious setback to efforts to stop torture during the period under study. Pursuant to agreements signed in 1982 and 1984 between the government and the International Committee of the Red Cross (ICRC), the ICRC is authorized to conduct regular visits both to penitentiary prisons and to DIRCOTE headquarters, in addition to providing emergency relief to the civilian population of Ayacucho. With regard to DIRCOTE, however, the program has been indefinitely suspended since April 1987. At first, the Ministry of Interior used a peculiar argument to justify reneging on its commitment: then-Minister Barsallo said that the newly enacted Law 24,700 gave the prosecutor the direction of investigations, and that only the *Fiscalía* could authorize visits to DIRCOTE. But the object of ICRC visits is by no means to participate in criminal investigations; the purpose is solely to give confidential advice to the Ministry of Interior about conditions of detention and potential mistreatment of detainees. Hugo Denegri, the Prosecutor General (*Fiscal de la Nación*), for his part, advised that the prosecutors were not entitled to grant permission for ICRC visits, although he would permit them to say that they had no objection to such visits. The result was a stalemate.

The officer who was then in charge of DIRCOTE, General Fernando Reyes Roca, is today the Chief of PIP. Americas Watch met with him and several advisors, as well as with the Minister of Interior, Admiral Juan Soria. In these interviews, as well as in those held with Foreign Minister Gonzales Posada, Prime Minister Villanueva and Minister of Justice Carrillo, Americas Watch insisted on the need to correct this serious flaw in the system to protect human rights. In the majority of countries where the ICRC visits security-related prisoners, its access is not limited to penitentiaries but extends also to pre-trial detention centers such as DIRCOTE. This is true both in Chile and, since June 1988 when ICRC visits began, in Cuba. As far as Americas Watch knows, the

ICRC is denied access to pre-trial detention centers in only Nicaragua and Peru. We have repeatedly urged the Nicaraguan government to allow such access.*

In our conversations with high government officials we were left with the clear impression that the government is not contemplating any change in this wrongheaded decision. We were told that the visiting program was suspended because the ICRC wanted "privileges" such as interviews with detainees without witnesses, which DIRCOTE refused to honor, supposedly because of security concerns, and because the ICRC wrote "disagreeable" reports about events in DIRCOTE. But an interview without witnesses is essential for receiving a candid account, and, in any event, ICRC reports to the government are absolutely confidential. Since the stated objections to ICRC visits appear to be objections to standard procedures that the ICRC follows throughout the world, the reasoning behind the suspension is particularly unfortunate. It implies that the program was suspended because in fact it did help avoid torture and improve conditions of detention.

In the emergency zone, even when the ICRC had permission to visit penal centers and to provide relief assistance, access was forbidden to military facilities where security-related prisoners were held. Since June 1988, all ICRC activities in the emergency zone have been completely forbidden; as a result, the ICRC presence in Peru is now restricted to prison visits (except in Ayacucho) and to relief assistance in San Martín. The programs to provide officers and troops with instruction on international humanitarian law standards have also been suspended. In previous years, some such classes were given to PIP and the Guardia Civil (GC), but talks aimed at extending these to Army personnel failed, even though such an extension was supported by the Center for Higher Military Studies (CAEM). ICRC proposals to provide emergency assistance to the displaced population in the emergency zone and to combat

---

*   See Americas Watch, <u>Report on Human Rights in Nicaragua 1987-88</u>, New York, August 1988, and several previous reports. Starting in December 1987, Americas Watch and other international organizations have been allowed visits to El Chipote in Managua, a pretrial detention center; similar requests to visit DIRCOTE facilities have not been granted.

epidemics in the Apurímac river valley have also been rejected because military authorities refused to grant the necessary permission.

C.   Extra-Judicial Executions

1.   Executions by the Military

With painful regularity, Peruvian public opinion has been jolted by news about massacres of peasants and the discovery of clandestine burial grounds. Except for the events in the prisons of Lima and Callao on June 19, 1988, all of these massacres have taken place in the emergency zone. From the killing of journalists in Uchuraccay to the Cayara massacre described below, there has been a painful succession of episodes in places whose names have now become familiar to Peruvians: Soccos, Pucayacu, Accomarca, Umaru-Bella Vista. In each of these cases there has been some responsibility by government forces. In Uchuraccay, journalists were killed by villagers who had just organized a civil patrol under orders of the Army. In Soccos, civilian courts finally convicted an officer and several members of the GC for the massacre. In the other cases, Army or Marine troops were responsible, but the investigations are still mired in the military courts which have assumed jurisdiction over the cases.

Americas Watch believes that indiscriminate killings are not necessarily being used by the Peruvian government as a tactical weapon of counter-insurgency, as is, in our judgment, the methodology of disappearances. But it is nonetheless evident that the officers charged with leading the war effort in the field occasionally do resort to the murder of civilians, without expectation of incurring punishment. In the cases mentioned, indiscriminate killings have been reprisals for Sendero ambushes. Even in the cases in which the Sendero attack could not have taken place without civilian support or silence, the indiscriminate killing of civilians violates the most fundamental principles of the laws of war, as well as the most honorable traditions of any self-respecting Army. Furthermore, the repetition of this irrational reaction is morally bankrupt and politically stupid, because it breeds hostility against the armed forces and facilitates continued recruitment by Sendero.

In the period covered by this report, Americas Watch has learned of one massacre committed by the Army, under the responsibility of the Political-Military Command of Ayacucho:

On May 13, 1988, a Sendero contingent ambushed 20 Army men in Erusco, province of Cangallo, Ayacucho. They detonated dynamite placed on the road and fired from trenches built alongside it. Several Senderistas participated; four were killed in the ensuing battle. The Army suffered the death of a captain and three soldiers.

The next day, the Army went into Cayara, the village closest to Erusco. According to witnesses, they killed the first dweller they found; they then went to the village church, where they found five men who were disassembling a makeshift altar, and shot them on the spot. The Army troops then assembled the villagers in the main square, waiting for the men to return from their work in the nearby fields. Young men and adults were separated from women and children and, in the presence of the latter, were forced to lie down. The soldiers then killed them using bayonets and farming tools. The total number of villagers murdered is between 28 and 31. The soldiers then buried the corpses nearby.

On May 18, the Army returned to Cayara and established a permanent base in the schoolhouse, consisting of some 20 men. That day, General Valdivia, Chief of the Political-Military Command of Ayacucho, read aloud a list of names of Cayara residents, presumably sought as subversives. The same list was later published by *Oiga*, a Lima magazine that frequently reflects the views of hard-liners in the armed forces. Some of the persons in the list were arrested that day and have since disappeared. The corpses of three of them were found in early August.

A few days later, Cayara neighbors arrived in Ayacucho and recounted these events. The Provincial Council of Huamanga (city council) issued a public statement, and the Lima news media then started reporting on the story. As is frequently the case, the initial account contained certain inaccuracies, such as a figure of 50 dead and a report of aerial bombing of the village. On the basis of those inaccuracies, the government attempted to deny that the entire episode had taken place. The essentials of the story, however, as described above, have been amply verfified by a variety of independent investigations conducted afterwards.

The first attempts to investigate the events were resisted by the Ayacucho Political-Military Command, which prohibited journalists, congressmen and the prosecutor-commissioner from travelling to Cayara. By the time those missions arrived in Cayara, the bodies were no longer in the burial sites identified by the witnesses, although Prosecutor Escobar was able to establish that those sites contained human traces (blood stains, hair) that were consistent with the witnesses' account.

On August 10, 1988, the villagers found the hidden remains of three persons in a place called Pucutuqasa, four hours from Cayara. Prosecutor Escobar exhumed the bodies and identified them as Alejandro Echeqaya Garay, Samuel García Palomino and Jovita García Suárez. All three had been detained in the May 18 raid led by General Valdivia.

> According to press accounts, the team led by Prosecutor Escobar took away the remains of Jovita García Suárez, but left the other two corpses behind for lack of transportation facilities. Nonetheless, clothing and other distinguishing marks allowed Flavia García, Jovita's sister, to make a positive identification of all three corpses. When investigators returned a few days later, the two corpses had been taken away and hidden again. According to press accounts, General Valdivia demanded that the police officer who went with Escobar report to the General about the *Fiscal's* findings. Senator Melgar then proceeded to accuse Escobar of conducting an illegal exhumation, allegedly for lack of witnesses, although the Code of Criminal Procedures clearly permits this in exceptional circumstances. The autopsy revealed that García Suárez was pregnant at the time of her death, and that her body had fractured limbs and a shattered cranium. As the possible cause of death, the autopsy gave two alternatives: the shattered cranium or a stab wound to the heart. In a new effort at disinformation, the Army said that Jovita García Suárez had been an Army informer and that Sendero had killed her.*

The new theft of the remains, and Senator Melgar's formal accusation against Prosecutor Escobar, bizarre as they may seem, are designed to make the investigation into these killings founder for lack of judicially admissible evidence.

A recent attempted murder has also shaken Peruvian public opinion and elicited international concern:**

> Sonia Muñoz de Yangali, a resident of Churkampa, Huancavelica, was arrested on May 18, 1988, by the Army; a few hours later three shots were fired at her at close range and

---

*   "Cuerpos que deambulan," Caretas, August 22, 1988; "Ya no están," Sí, August 22, 1988.

**   Amnesty International, Peru: Violations of Human Rights in the Emergency Zones, London, August 1988.

she was left for dead on a road near her community. The woman, however, managed to survive and, apparently with the help of neighbors, walked first to Huanta, then to Ayacucho, and eventually travelled to Lima, where she was given medical attention at a prestigious clinic. Dr. Esteban Roca conducted an operation and took out three bullets that were lodged in her cranium and shoulders; miraculously, they had not hurt any important organ. Dr. Roca publicly confirmed that the shots had been fired at close range, and delivered the bullets, with his testimony, to Prosecutor General Hugo Denegri. In July, we received reports that several residents of Churkampa who had assisted Yangali in her flight had disappeared following their arrest by security forces.

The Yangali case confirms that the fate of many of the disappeared is to be killed by their captors. Prosecutor Carlos Escobar has been able to clarify several cases of disappearances by locating the remains of the victims.

On August 28, 1987, members of an Army unit called "Los Linces" (lynx) arrested Fermín Yukra Kiwe, Néstor and Ricardo Amau Quispe, Mardonio Quispe Romero, Anselmo and Marcelino Medina Jorge, and Teodoro Naupa Quispe, all in the community of Santa Rosa, Ayna district, province of La Mar, Ayacucho. The mother of two of them, Julia Jorge de Medina, told Prosecutor Escobar that the arrest had taken place in her presence, that she had followed the soldiers and found that five of the kidnapped men, including her two sons, had been murdered. A justice of the peace and a health technician found the bodies and identified the Medina Jorge brothers in a place called Bajíos de Patacocha. The two Amau Quispe brothers escaped from their captors and, after remaining in hiding for several weeks, were evacuated from the area by Prosecutor Escobar, as witnesses under his protection, when the investigative team visited the area.

2. Executions by the Comando Rodrigo Franco

In addition to these abuses at the hands of uniformed soldiers, a new shadowy group recently has emerged on the scene. Its first victim was Manuel Febres, an attorney, who was murdered on July 28, 1988 in Lima. One of the most prominent members of the Association of Democratic Lawyers, he is perhaps best known for his defense of Osmán Morote Barrionuevo, regarded as

Sendero's top-ranking leader in jail. In the first of several cases against Morote, as noted above, Febres obtained an acquittal. The trial attracted great attention and Febres's face and name became familiar to most Peruvians.

Febres was kidnapped in the morning of July 28, only a few hours before the President's annual address to Congress, in which he criticized Morote's acquittal and announced tougher legislation against "subversives." Febres was seized at 8:30 a.m. near his house in a central neighborhood of the Miraflores district. At 9:50 the same day, a taxi driver discovered his body at the exit for the Herradura beach. He had been shot seven times. His corpse was identified that evening by his relatives.

The ballistics test showed Febres to have been shot by 9 mm bullets, a calibre used by many different weapons. He was shot from the back, as he ran, with an automatic pistol firing shots one at a time. The fact that under the circumstances he was hit seven times suggests that the shooter was a highly skilled marksman.* His killers must also have known that he displayed personal and intellectual leadership among his colleagues in the Association of Democratic Lawyers, the members of which have been threatened and harassed in the past because press and government circles regard them as linked to Sendero Luminoso. One member, José Vázquez Huayca, was captured in 1986 and remains disappeared, as Americas Watch reported in 1987.

The "Rodrigo Franco Command" claimed responsibility for the murder of Febres in a message sent to the press. The group was unknown before this action, but has since committed other acts of violence and threatened several public figures.

This murder deserves condemnation not only in its own right but also because its perpetrators seek to discourage lawyers from taking up unpopular cases. Access to counsel is a fundamental right that must be enjoyed by all defendants. That right is threatened if lawyers who defend so-called "subversives" are thereby identified with the acts of their clients. Little is known so far about Febres's killers, but their apparent conception of lawyers who defend alleged "subversives" is, unfortunately, widely held in police circles. At a meeting with PIP chiefs in July, a close advisor to General Reyes repeatedly told Americas Watch that lawyers are an integral part of Sendero's structure.

---

*   "Caso Febres: La Pista de la Bala," Caretas, August 8, 1988.

52

The killers of Manuel Febres adopted the name of Rodrigo Franco, a well-known lawyer who was a member of the governing party and an activist in the conservative Catholic movement Opus Dei. Franco was killed by Sendero in 1987, in his house and in front of his family; at the time he was the president of a large state enterprise. Franco's family has repudiated the actions of the new terrorist group.* In the message distributed to the press, the new group stated that it was formed by citizens who are "tired of Alan García's demagoguery and of the indecisiveness of the security forces," and announced that "for each mayor, soldier or policeman murdered, a Sendero leader or a leader of the groups that support and protect Sendero will die."**

A few days later, the Comando Rodrigo Franco blew up the grave of Edith Lagos, a young Sendero woman from Ayacucho who died fighting security forces and has since become a political symbol in Ayacucho. Later, the Comando Rodrigo Franco threatened the life of Prosecutor Carlos Escobar, who, as noted, has been commissioned to investigate disappearances in Ayacucho as well as the Cayara massacre, and has done a highly commendable job of pursuing these cases. The decision to target Escobar can only be interpreted as an attempt to discourage investigations that might establish the responsibility of government forces for ghastly abuses. We have learned that members of Congress have also received threats, as has journalist Luis Morales, *El Diario*'s correspondent in Ayacucho. Another threat, of great concern to Americas Watch, was made against Monsignor Luis Bambarén, Bishop of Chimbote, and one of the best known leaders of the Peruvian Church, who until recently was head of the Episcopal Commission on Social Action (CEAS), one of the country's most prestigious human rights organizations.

The Comando Rodrigo Franco also claimed credit for the murder of two persons linked to the MRTA, who were negotiating the payment of ransom in exchange for the release of a general kidnapped by that insurgent group. In addition, the Comando Rodrigo Franco bombed the house and office of a

---

*   Resumen Semanal, DESCO, Lima, No.480.

**   Ibid

prominent Ayacucho lawyer, Mario Cavalcanti, the vice-chairman of the Ayacucho Bar Association, who is well known for his representation of persons accused of terrorist activities. In October, as this report was being completed, the Comando Rodrigo Franco murdered two trade union leaders of the mineworkers, in separate incidents.

The origin of the Comando Rodrigo Franco is unknown, although there has been much speculation in this regard in the Peruvian press. The political bent of its victims, coupled with its daring daylight kidnapping of Manuel Febres, reflects a sense of impunity on the part of the perpetrators that may be suggestive of some sort of complicity with the military.

Regardless of its origins, however, many analysts agree that with Febres's murder, the Comando Rodrigo Franco has brought the country's human rights situation to a breaking point. This may well lead to the development of criminal gangs such as the "Triple A" in Argentina in the 1970's and the death squads of El Salvador and Guatemala. Indeed, in the southern city of Ica, Congressman Julio Renán Raffo, of the United Left, and several university and municipal officials linked to that coalition, have been threatened by a secret "Comando" calling itself "Manuel Santan Chiri," after an APRA leader in Ica who was murdered in 1986. If such spiraling violence is to be avoided, the Peruvian government has a most serious responsibility to clarify any possible relationship between government forces and the Comando Rodrigo Franco terrorist group, and must make renewed efforts to identify, arrest and prosecute its members.

VII. FREEDOM OF EXPRESSION

Despite the deteriorating human rights conditions in other areas which we point out in other sections of this report, Peru continued to enjoy broad freedom of the press in the year under study. A large number of publications are available to the public, albeit of widely differing quality. The state of emergency that is in effect in several areas does not affect the circulation of newspapers and magazines. Radio and television also participate freely in the debate on the country's most important problems. Americas Watch does, however, have some concerns about freedom of expression, even in this generally favorable context.

After several changes in ownership, *El Diario*, a Lima daily, has become Sendero's semi-official, if not official, mouthpiece. Each issue presents the version of events most clearly favorable to Sendero, and often clarifies whether a specific terrorist action is to be attributed to Sendero or not. On July 31, 1988, it published a special 48-page edition consisting of a long, exclusive interview with Abimael Guzmán (aka "Camarada Gonzalo"), Sendero's top leader.*

Because of *El Diario*'s new role, numerous officials have called for its closure, including President García in his speech of July 28, when he alluded to those who abuse democracy. As noted previously, Americas Watch objects to proposals to criminalize "apologia of terrorism," because the text of the proposed law is so vague that it threatens to chill legitimate speech and press commentary well beyond the advocacy of violence.

It should be obvious that our position on this topic constitutes no defense of *El Diario*'s practices; we have no admiration for its editorial policies or journalistic style. We do, however, defend the right of *El Diario*, and everyone

---

* "Presidente Gonzalo Rompe el Silencio," by Luis Arce Borja and Janet Talavera Sánchez, El Diario, July 31, 1988.

else, to publish their non-violent ideas in the press without prior censorship and without the threat of sanctions.

In August 1988, the police arrested Luis Arce Borja, the editor of *El Diario*. He was released within a few hours, but rearrested a few days later, this time on a court order. Upon his arrest, Americas Watch sent a letter to President García, inquiring about the reasons for the detention. It appears that Arce is accused of defrauding the government by illegally selling newsprint that is imported with customs benefits. A judge has ruled that no prosecution is warranted and ordered Arce released; however, a prosecutor has appealed, and the case is now before the 11th Tribunal in Lima.* In the meantime, *El Diario* has temporarily suspended publication.

The Political-Military Command of Ayacucho has continued its policy of restricting access by journalists to rural areas in the emergency zone, even though, as we said in our 1987 report, the policy is an abuse of the exceptional powers contemplated in the Constitution for a state of emergency. The restrictions have hampered both national and international journalists in their efforts to investigate acts of violence by both sides to the conflict. Besides posing a serious limitation on the right to information, this practice contributes to popular distrust of official news stories and encourages exaggeration and myth to prevail over truth.

---

* See "Nuevas de El Diario," <u>Caretas</u>, September 12, 1988, page 70.

VIII. RESTRICTIONS ON HUMAN RIGHTS AND HUMANITARIAN ORGANIZATIONS

The restriction on movement in certain rural areas of Ayacucho applies not only to journalists but also to relief organizations which provide irreplaceable humanitarian services. Our 1987 report discussed the restrictions imposed on *Medecins Sans Frontieres* (MSF) and its Peruvian counterpart, *Centro de Educación y Cultura Andina* (CEDCA); first, they were prohibited from leaving the Huamanga city limits, then, some months later, all their activities were banned. We also reported on similar restrictions imposed by military authorities on the ICRC. In March 1988, after protracted negotiations, the ICRC obtained a new permit to provide assistance to displaced persons in the Department of Ayacucho, which it did for the following three months. After the Cayara massacre in May, the ICRC asked for permission to go to the village and provide emergency aid to survivors, but the request was denied. In late June, ICRC representatives in Huamanga were given notice that their permit to work in the emergency zone was indefinitely suspended. No reason was given. The notice had no qualification, so presumably it applies also to ICRC visits to security-related inmates in eight prisons in the zone.

Around the same time, other organizations that deliver services in the emergency zone suffered a similar curtailment of their work. Another French organization, *Medecins du Monde* (MDM), and the relief arm of the local Catholic Church, *Organización de Acción Social del Arzobispado* (OASA), also received orders not to travel to rural areas. Both organizations performed an invaluable service by providing medical attention, food, clothing and housing to civilians displaced or affected by the war; this population is now deprived of such basic services.

These restrictions were not immediately reported in the Peruvian press. In the course of a parliamentary hearing in July, Prime Minister Armando Villanueva received a question about the status of the ICRC in Ayacucho. He answered that military authorities had banned MSF after discovering that MSF medicine had ended up in Sendero's hands, but noted that there were no restrictions with regard to the ICRC. In a private meeting with Americas Watch, the Prime Minister repeated the same answer. With respect to the ICRC, the Prime Minister is in error: since June 1988, the ICRC has not been allowed to perform any activity in the emergency zone.

MSF no longer has any presence in Peru. Although we are not familiar with the circumstances leading to its expulsion, we note that, even if the Prime Minister's reasons were correct, they would be insufficient to justify depriving the Andean population of such an important service. As stated to us and to the Peruvian Congress, the decision is also in violation of Peru's obligations under international humanitarian law, which prohibits any interference with medical assistance not only to civilians but also to belligerents.

As we said in our 1987 report, we are left with the impression that the real reason for these restrictions is the desire to engage in repressive acts outside the presence of witnesses. That such motives are allowed to prevail over the need to address the suffering of victims is further evidence of how irrational the strategy of counter-insurgency has become. The same criteria were applied to our own visit to Ayacucho of July 8 and 9, 1988 (see our letter to President García in the appendix). PIP agents visited Juan E. Méndez at his hotel and inquired about his activities. When he said he intended to go to nearby Huanta, the officers said he had to request a permit from the Political-Military Command. Méndez went to the Command's headquarters at the Los Cabitos military base in Huamanga, where he was received by the Chief, General José Valdivia. Valdivia not only refused to grant permission to visit Huanta, but also ordered Méndez not to perform any activity in Huamanga and to return to Lima. According to Valdivia, Méndez should have obtained a special permit from the Joint Command of the Armed Forces in Lima before travelling to Ayacucho.

Méndez informed General Valdivia that he had told the Peruvian government of Americas Watch's interest in visiting Ayacucho, both in discussions with the Embassy in Washington and in the course of interviews with four Cabinet members in Lima: Prime Minister Villanueva, Foreign Minister Gonzales Posada, Justice Minister Carrillo and Interior Minister Soria. In none of these discussions was he ever told that he needed a special permit to go to

Ayacucho. This argument failed to move General Valdivia, however; he insisted on his version of the rules and ordered Méndez to stay at his hotel until the next morning's flight to Lima. Later that day, an aide to Valdivia ratified his order by telephone, presumably after consultation with the Joint Command in Lima.

Freedom of movement is one of the four rights that can legally be suspended during a state of emergency. However, the authorities have established no regulations setting forth criteria for the enforcement of restrictions on movement, with the result that the Political-Military Command's decisions to prevent journalists, relief organizations and human rights groups from travelling in the region are made in a completely arbitrary and discriminatory fashion. In that sense, the restrictions as applied go beyond the legitimate exercise of the derogation principle of international law, because they are not rationally related to the dangerous situation giving rise to the state of emergency.*

At the same time as our expulsion from Ayacucho there was another event that we consider more threatening to the freedoms of association and expression. On July 9, 1988, under orders from the Political-Military Command, PIP forces arrested Father Carlos Gallagher and lay social workers Pilar Coll, Susana González and Elsa Ballón. The three were in Ayacucho on a mission of CEAS, the human rights arm of the Catholic Bishops, to monitor the situation in the zone of emergency. On the same day, PIP arrested Guadalupe Ccalloc-cunto and German citizen Rainer Uhle, both of whom are affiliated with the Ayacucho office of *Servicio de Paz y Justica para América Latina* (SERPAJ). After their interrogation at PIP headquarters, four of the five were released some 30 hours after their arrest; Uhle spent a full three days in custody. Prosecutors and the judge found that there was no reason whatsoever to arrest these people. SERPAJ-Ayacucho is an affiliate of the organization led at the Latin American level by Nobel Peace Prize winner Adolfo Pérez Esquivel, and it works primarily with victims of repression. CEAS is the official entity for conducting the pastoral work of the Catholic Church of Peru, and its human rights

---

* Article 4 of the International Covenant on Civil and Political Rights and Article 27 of the American Convention on Human Rights allow the suspension of certain rights "...to the extent strictly required by the exigencies of the situation..."

office has rightfully earned great recognition throughout the hemisphere. Pilar Coll is also the director of the *Coordinadora Nacional de Derechos Humanos*, an institution that spans the several independent human rights organizations of Peru.

There is no recent precedent in Peru for the arrest of such people whose human rights work includes the unmistakable condemnation of political violence of any sort. Since there was no reasonable basis or probable cause for it, one must conclude that the motivation was to discourage human rights monitoring in the emergency zone. National authorities must urgently affirm the right to conduct such monitoring without interference, and offer guarantees to independent institutions to continue to perform such work. The detentions in Ayacucho constitute an attack on the human rights movement of Peru, a movement which was launched by institutions with a clearly established democratic character and a sense of responsibility in the conduct of their humanitarian calling.

More recently, a document issued by the Armed Forces accused a legal assistant with APRODEH, who had made inquiries about security-related detentions, of seeking to discredit the Armed Forces. Civilian authorities must rectify such attitudes on the part of the security forces against human rights monitoring.

The most serious attacks against those who defend security-related prisoners have been suffered by the *Asociación de Abogados Democráticos*, as we noted in our 1987 report. As discussed above, the kidnappers and murderers of attorney Manuel Febres, that Association's most distinguished lawyer, are so far unknown, but the victim's background and the fact that his kidnapping took place in a busy street corner in front of numerous witnesses suggest a sense of impunity on the part of the perpetrators that only some sort of complicity with sectors of the security forces can provide. The role of high military authorities in the other, less severe actions against human rights monitors is open and public. Americas Watch considers all these actions to be serious attacks against those who defend the rule of law. It is urgent to put a stop to these actions and to discipline those who want to blur distinctions between human rights monitors and those who use violence against the state.

60

IX. THE ROLE OF OTHER BRANCHES OF GOVERNMENT IN PROTECTING HUMAN RIGHTS

A.   Congress

1.   The Ames Commission

The Congress of Peru managed in the last year to produce an intelligent, thorough and fair investigation into a very difficult human rights matter. That this is one of very few bright spots in a dismal picture does not diminish its significance: it shows that it is indeed possible for a parliamentary inquiry to get at hard truths and to produce salutary results.

After the killing of hundreds of rioting inmates in three prisons on June 19, 1986, President García promised a full investigation. In the Senate, a special commission of inquiry was set up, and the chair was offered to the opposition. After Senator (and former General) Jorge Fernández Maldonado declined the chair, the Commission remained dormant for several months. In 1987 it finally started its investigation, under the chairmanship of Senator Rolando Ames, an independent elected on the United Left ticket. Our 1987 report was published just as the findings of the so-called Ames Report were being made public. Almost a year later, Americas Watch believes it necessary to take a closer look not only at the report itself, but also at the workings of the Ames Commission, because they provide insight into the usefulness of parliamentary work in the promotion of human rights.

The Executive Branch granted the Commission full access to government documents, even those that previously had been classified. The Commission was also allowed to visit the sites of the events without restrictions, and to question key actors. Undoubtedly, such unqualified cooperation on the part of the García administration was a key to the success of the inquiry. As a result, many documents and transcripts describing meetings at the Council of Ministers, as well as confidential reports from the Joint Command of the Armed Forces, have now been placed in the public domain for future consultation. On

61

the basis of that wealth of information, the Commission's staff was able to provide a careful, scrupulous reconstruction of the massacre, in which most of the mutineers were murdered after they surrendered, as well as of the decision-making process that led to this tragedy.

In the end, the Commission produced two reports. The "majority report" was signed by the members belonging to the government party and its allies, and the "minority report" was signed by Senator Ames and the members belonging to opposition parties of the left and right. Interestingly, however, both reports were identical in the factual description of the events and differed only in the political conclusions and recommendations for congressional action. Both reports described the Cabinet's and the President's involvement in the events. On that basis, Senator Ames and the minority proposed that Congress invoke the constitutional proceeding for the filing of criminal charges against high government officials, i.e., a vote by both houses of Congress to initiate such judicial actions. This system, known in Peru as *antejuicio constitucional*, is similar to the impeachment process in the United States, except that, in Peru, if Congress had gone along with the recommendation, the criminal prosecution against President García would have taken place only at the end of his term, in 1990.

Besides President García, Senator Ames and the minority recommended the same action against the Ministers present at the Cabinet meetings where the decisions were made; the *Fiscal de la Nación*, César Elejalde, and the Vice-Minister of Interior, Agustín Mantilla, who were physically present in El Frontón; the Director of Prisons (INPE); and officers and troops who participated in the killings. The majority report exculpated the most prominent members of the government, and restricted its accusations to the members of the military who participated in the massacres, *Fiscal* Elejalde (who must also be impeached first), and the Director of Prisons. Congress has not yet acted on the recommendation to impeach *Fiscal* Elejalde, even though his successor as Prosecutor General has endorsed such action. Charges are pending in civilian courts against Vice-Minister Mantilla and the Director of Prisons. With regard to the military, the highest court of military jurisdiction, the *Consejo Supremo de las Fuerzas Armadas*, announced in July that formal charges have been filed against officers and troops involved in one of the prison massacres at

Lurigancho. A spokesman for the Supreme Council told Americas Watch in July that the preparation of cases against those involved in massacres at two other prisons, El Frontón and Santa Bárbara, were still pending.

The report establishes that for months the prisons had been allowed to drift in a chaotic and dangerous direction, and that information given to the public during the events was deliberately distorted to exaggerate the importance of the mutinies, thereby making harsh measures appear justified. It also shows that high government officials — Vice-Minister Mantilla and military chiefs — deliberately and illegally prevented judges and prosecutors from fulfilling their legal duties. It establishes that President García's government made decisions that were inconsistent with its duty to protect human life and reckless, at the very least, in not foreseeing the resulting tragedy. The President himself insisted on putting down the riots in the shortest possible time, even though there appeared to be no imminent danger to the lives of hostages or any other reason to hasten the use of force.

The force used by the military to put down the riot was disproportionate to any measure of the actual danger. In only one of the prisons did the inmates have firearms, and then only three; in the other two prisons the inmates had none. The security forces used machine guns, rocket launchers, bazookas, 81mm cannons, plastic explosives and dynamite.* The report also found that some members of the security forces executed inmates after they had surrendered. In Lurigancho, at least 90 of the rioting inmates were murdered with a shot to the back of their head, after they had given up. No one survived in Lurigancho. In El Frontón, the Navy blew up the Blue Cellblock, knowing there were still inmates alive inside. Thirty-five inmates (of around 140) were taken alive in El Frontón. Some witnesses suggest that in El Frontón as well, some of the surrendering inmates were murdered by their captors, and Naval authorities have not denied such allegations.

---

*   The report from the Joint Command says that Vice-Minister Mantilla gave the order to initiate the attack against the Blue Cellblock of El Frontón, which began with the firing of two rockets against the outside wall of the building (Informe al Congreso sobre los Sucesos de los Penales [Ames Report], p. 145).

One of the most serious findings of the Ames report is that the government initially tried to cover up the crimes committed by the security forces. The President and his Cabinet learned immediately about the number of casualties in each of the prisons, as well as the lack of survivors in Lurigancho. Instead of ordering an investigation, however, the President commended the job done by the Joint Command.* The President did later make a formal criminal complaint, alluding only to Lurigancho, although by then it was clear that illegal acts had taken place in the other two prisons as well.

The report states that Supreme Decree 006-86-JUS, issued on June 19, was manifestly unconstitutional. The report also criticized the decree because it purported to apply to events retroactively. The decree established that military courts would have jurisdiction, when in fact only the Supreme Court is entitled to make that jurisdictional decision; and it attempted to place civilians under military jurisdiction which is explicitly forbidden by the Peruvian Constitution.

The parliamentary debate that followed the Ames Report was weak and discouraging. Although the Congress approved the majority report, the public was encouraged to see that the institutions had served a useful function. There was a general sense that the resulting investigation, though damaging to

---

*   The transcript of the Cabinet meeting of June 19, 1986 shows that the President reported as follows:

    "As a result of the actions, we have the total destruction of Blue Cellblock, with around thirty subversives having surrendered; the corpses of another twenty have been found, the rest are under the debris, in the galleries built by the inmates themselves and which were used as a sort of cells for those not yet reaching an adequate level of indoctrination. At the Lurigancho prison it has been possible to rescue the one hostage, with the result of more than one hundred dead. In Santa Bárbara two prisoners have died and there is a certain number of wounded.

    "The balance of the action is lamentable, but it serves to show to the country that the government has imposed its authority.

    "The President expresses his commendation to the Joint Command of the Armed Forces for the efficient compliance with the orders of the government. It is also pointed out that, according to Law 24,150 which regulates states of exception, jurisdiction in this matter lies with military courts; therefore, it was decided that civilian judges would not be allowed to enter the prisons nor the nearby premises, starting that same afternoon; the prisons are declared Restricted Military Zones, and access to civilians is thus prohibited."
    (Translated from the transcripts, Ames Report, pp. 329-30).

important officials, strengthened the democratic process by showing that parliamentary bodies can serve effectively. The full Ames Report, with important documentary annexes, was published in book form under the joint sponsorship of the Lima Bar Association, the College of Physicians, the College of Journalists, the Peruvian Association of Studies and Research for Peace, APRODEH, CAJ, IDL, COMISEDH, the National Coordinating Body for Human Rights, and trade and peasant union federations. The Peruvian College of Engineers endorsed the conclusions of expert engineering witnesses who had demonstrated that the Navy had demolished the Blue Cellblock.* Many important institutions of civil society expressed high regard for the Ames Report. International associations and inter-governmental organizations for the protection of human rights should disseminate the results of this important inquiry.

2. The Melgar Commission

When the Cayara massacre came to light, the President and the Minister of Justice invited the President of the Bar Association, Raúl Ferrero, and Lima Auxiliary Bishop Mons. Augusto Beuzeville to visit the village with government authorities. According to Ferrero and Mons. Beuzeville, they received testimonies from villagers that an Army unit had committed crimes against the peasants.

Although at first the government-party members of both houses argued against proposals to investigate the massacre (Senators Carlos Melgar and Quintana Gurt asked for more time to receive Army reports), the Congress finally approved the formation of two Special Commissions of Inquiry to look into the massacre; although one Commission was established for each house, the two were supposed to work together and share information. Senator Melgar and Representative Jorge Sánchez Farfán, both of the APRA party, were named to chair the two commissions. The Cayara massacre was committed on May 14, the commissions were appointed on May 23, and they met for the first time on May 27. This deliberately slow pace continued thereafter, particularly

---

*   Naval authorities had insisted that the mutineers themselves had blown up the building.

on the Senate side. Other members of the panel, both from the majority and the minority, publicly criticized Senator Melgar's delaying tactics.* As of this writing, there have been plenty of personal opinions and controversial actions, but no reports from either panel.

Members of the Senate Commission decided to travel to the site on their own, without waiting for Senator Melgar. Despite initial restrictions imposed by the military command, Senator Mohme and others were able to obtain a credible version of events. The House Commission traveled to Cayara early on. Chairman Sánchez Farfán, however, seemed from the beginning inclined to find reasons to believe the version of events proposed by the Army, no matter how unlikely.** In mid-June, Senator Melgar finally went to Ayacucho with his staff. According to journalists, other members of the Commission, and observers, the delegation spent three days in Ayacucho, mostly talking to military authorities and avoiding direct contact with witnesses and relatives of the victims.

At the time Prosecutor Escobar had gathered more information about the massacre than any other public official. Senator Melgar met with him for about 40 minutes, but spent almost the entire interview questioning Escobar's credentials and his appointment. According to Escobar, "it appeared that the facts themselves did not interest him [Melgar] much."*** At that meeting, the Chairman of the Senate Commission asked Escobar for the names of witnesses and other results of the prosecutorial investigation, all of which was strictly confidential until that time. A few days later, five persons disappeared in Cayara after their arrest by the Army; one of them was a key witness to Escobar's investigation, and three of the others were his parents and sister.

Besides apparently helping to obstruct the inquiry, Senator Melgar issued a stream of outrageous statements to the press. In one interview, he said

---

* Statements by Senators Gustavo Mohme and Ruperto Figueroa to the press, La República, May 27, 1988.

** Meeting with Americas Watch in Washington, June 22, 1988.

*** Interview by Mariella Balbi, La República, June 11, 1988.

that he had not interviewed witnesses to the massacre because he was not "a *chulillo* of theirs to go around running after witnesses."* In the same interview, the Senator said: "I ask of those Amnesty International imbeciles why don't they protest the swindle perpetrated by Messrs. Reagan and Gorbachov. They are imbeciles and corrupt because they are telling the world that Peru is a country of genocides and that should not be done, that is offensive." Americas Watch deplores these verbal excesses.

The work of the Melgar Commission has elicited widespread and justified criticism.** In glaring contrast with the Ames Commission, Senator Melgar has directed his investigatory zeal primarily toward covering up the facts, protecting the possible culprits, particularly General José Valdivia, and obstructing the independent investigation carried out by the Prosecutor. In addition to the attitudes described in the preceding paragraphs, the Senator has more recently attempted to foil Prosecutor Escobar's investigation into the above-noted discovery of three corpses belonging to persons arrested by the Army in the wake of the Cayara massacre. After Escobar's life was threatened by the Comando Rodrigo Franco terrorist organization, Senator Melgar said publicly that "if something happens to the *Fiscal*, then it happens; he would be replaced, that is the risk."*** This is more than callous disregard for life; it is an open and irresponsible invitation to criminal activity, unworthy of a high elected official.

As of this writing, no report of the Melgar Commission is expected any time soon. It appears that at least three separate reports are in preparation: one by Senator Melgar himself, another by an independent member, Senator Navarro Grau, and a third by two opposition members, Senators Mohme and Diez Canseco. Neither the House nor the Senate inquiries have helped to clarify the

---

*   La República, June 30, 1988. Chulillo is a derogatory term used to refer to the cholo or inhabitant of the Andes. In this context, it also refers to not being a servant.

**   An independent journal has stated: "It is true that Senator Melgar is prejudging the case and that his animosity against the prosecutor is unforgivable." Caretas, August 29, 1988.

***   "Fiscal del caso Cayara denuncia que ahora pretenden amedretarlo," La República, Aug. 23, 1988, p. 8.

events, although at least it can be said that travel by some members to the village itself prompted the citizens to come forward bravely with their testimonies. Senator Melgar has deliberately used his powers to cover up the episode and even to obstruct justice; his outrageous statements are calculated to prevent discovery of the truth and punishment of the murderers. The result discredits the parliamentary body and Peru's civilian institutions in general, further undermining democratic authority in Peru.

B.   The Judiciary

In the last year there has been some moderate progress in bringing to justice the perpetrators of human rights violations, mostly in connection with the facts disclosed by the Ames Report. A criminal prosecution is finally under way before the highest military court in regard to the murder of approximately one hundred inmates in Lurigancho prison in 1986. As noted, the riot of June 18 of that year was put down by the Army and by the Guardia Republicana (GR), a police body. The accusation by the military prosecutor* charges the officer in charge of the operation, Brigadier General Jorge Rabanal Portilla of the Army, with simple homicide, and requests the penalty of six years in prison. Colonel Rolando Cabezas, of the GR, is charged with aggravated murder, and the sentence requested is 25 years. Another 23 Army and GR officers are included in the accusation, all of them charged with simple homicide. Among them is General Máximo Martínez Lira, former Chief of the GR. Another 64 GR police agents are also charged with homicide, with requested penalties ranging from 6 to 25 years in prison. The case is now expected to go to trial before the Supreme Council.

By contrast, the investigation into the events of the same day at the island prison of El Frontón has advanced little. In that case, the investigation is directed against the Navy and police forces. The Naval prosecutor is not known to have taken any investigative or prosecutorial steps in this case. The lawyers

---

*   Dictamen Fiscal No. 088, Consejo Supremo de Justicia Militar, Sala de Guerra, Case Number 638-V-86.

for the Navy (*Cuerpo Jurídico de la Marina*) also refused to provide any information to the Ames Commission, in contrast to their colleagues in the Army legal office, which made all their files available.

As for the civilians implicated in those tragic events, in April 1988 the Prosecutor for Callao filed charges against former Vice-Minister of Interior Agustín Mantilla and the former Director of Prisons, charging them with homicide, usurping authority, using violence, and resisting authority (contempt) for having prevented the Director of El Frontón, the judges and the prosecutor who had come to the prison from exercising their respective legal roles while the riot was in progress.* As noted above, the prosecution of former Prosecutor General Elejalde has not started because Congress has not yet acted on the recommendation to impeach him first.

These few prosecutions are rare exceptions to a troubling impunity that the military enjoys for the hundreds of cases of summary execution, disappearance and torture committed by its forces. Military courts have been extremely lenient toward cases of human rights abuse, or have thwarted investigations by delaying the secret proceedings indefinitely. According to the Code of Military Justice, military jurisdiction attaches only when both the defendant and the victim are members of the military. Nonetheless, the Supreme Court has repeatedly assigned cases to the military courts when civilians are victims, as in the discovery of clandestine graves in Pucayacu and the murder of inmates in the Lima prisons.

Even in the Lurigancho case, although the Prosecutor's recent filing of charges is welcome, it comes more than two years after the event, and only after a conscientious parliamentary investigation placed overwhelming evidence of criminality before the public. We find, therefore, no reason to alter our opinion, expressed in previous reports, that in Peru, military jurisdiction has become a pretext for impunity rather than an effective means of exerting legal control over the armed forces. Congress has failed to act on a bill designed to attack this problem by redefining "military offenses" (*delito de función*), even though the

---

* Sí Magazine, No. 64, May 16, 1988.

proposal had been unanimously passed by the Senate. Ratifying the principles set forth in other laws, the proposed bill would establish that genocide, murder, rape, abduction and other common crimes are to be tried by civilian courts. The human rights community of Peru has strongly backed this legislative initiative.

From our point of view, punishment of those found guilty of human rights abuse is fundamental, not because of a need for revenge, but because the laws that those officials violate are meant to affirm essential values of democratic societies. For example, in punishing murder or disappearance, the law affirms the value of human life; in punishing torture, it affirms the value of physical and psychological integrity of the person. A society that wishes genuinely to affirm such fundamental values is obligated, for consistency's sake, to punish behavior that offends those values.* We are unwilling to accept that murder of civilians, disappearance and indiscriminate killing can be legitimate military actions, and for that reason we urge Congress to adopt the bill that would establish clear civilian jurisdiction over such crimes and restrict military court jurisdiction to truly military offenses.

C.   The Office of the Prosecutor General

Under Peru's Constitution, the *Fiscalía de la Nación* (Office of the Prosecutor General) is a separate branch of government, independent from the Executive as well as from the Judiciary. In addition to supervising all prosecutors throughout the country, the Prosecutor General acts as an Ombudsman, or "Defender of the People," to protect individual rights against abuses by the administration. In both roles, the proper and efficient work of the Office is essential for the protection of human rights. In our 1987 report, we expressed the hope that a meaningful improvement might result from the

---

*   See Marcelo Sancinetti, "Derechos Humanos en La Argentina Post-Dictatorial," LEA, Buenos Aires, 1988, p. 9; Article 2, International Covenant on Civil and Political Rights; Article 25, American Convention on Human Rights.

appointment of Hugo Denegri Cornejo as Prosecutor General.* Fortunately, we are in a position to say that in the year covered by this report, the Office of the Prosecutor General has given encouraging signs of concern for human rights.

Denegri's predecessor, César Elejalde Estenssoro, assumed a negative and counterproductive attitude toward the investigations into disappearances, presenting himself as an *a priori* defender of the prestige of the armed and security forces, and impugning the patriotism of those who filed complaints.** Today, many of the chronic problems of the Office still exist: inefficiency, lack of adequate training, and bureaucratic attitudes on the part of many officials. In many cases, these problems may well be compounded by corruption. With respect to human rights violations, however, the Office has begun to insist on bringing charges against agents of repression when evidence can be found, and it has consistently urged that those prosecutions be pursued before civilian courts. Unfortunately, the Supreme Court has almost invariably transferred these cases to military tribunals.

More important, the Office of the Prosecutor General has recently created a special mechanism to address disappearances, and the early results are exemplary. In mid-1987, the new *Fiscal de la Nación* created the position of Superior Prosecutor-Commissioner for the Investigation of Disappearances, and appointed prosecutor Carlos Escobar Pineda to fill it. Escobar moved to Ayacucho on July 4, 1987, with two adjunct prosecutors. This team's mission is to receive complaints about disappeared persons in the Ayacucho emergency zone, to investigate their whereabouts and legal status and, if the disappeared are found, to determine whether they should remain under arrest or be released. If the detainee is found in the custody of the Armed Forces, the Prosecutor orders that the prisoner be transferred to PIP facilities, because, although during

---

*   The Fiscalía is made up of four Supreme Prosecutors, who rotate every two years in the position of Prosecutor General. In each judicial district, the Office also has provincial, superior and adjunct prosecutors.

**   See: Ministerio Público, Fiscalía de la Nación, Memoria 1985, Lima, May 1986, pgs. 33 and 56-60.

71

the state of emergency the military may arrest persons, it may not hold them indefinitely. If evidence of the commission of offenses by security agents is gathered, the Prosecutor-Commissioner must ask a local prosecutor to file charges.

Escobar had to contend with complaints that had been filed with the Ayacucho Office in previous years, complaints filed in the preceding weeks or months (for which the victims might still be found alive), and new complaints. With regard to the first group, relatives were asked to reconfirm and update the information on file, and new inquiries were made. For the two other groups, Escobar's strategy is to act promptly: he sends urgent requests for information and immediately shows up at detention centers. PIP, GC and GR offices are obligated to cooperate with him, since police bodies are auxiliaries of the prosecution in the investigation of crimes. With respect to military units, the officer in charge generally refuses to grant access; Escobar then returns with a judge to conduct a judicial search.

In little more than a year (interrupted by other missions), Escobar's team has accumulated an impressive record of small victories. Roughly 50% of the complaints received have resulted in the reappearance of the victim, either in freedom or in acknowledged and regularized custody. In a small number of cases, corpses have been found. During certain periods, the success rate has been even higher. The team has been aggressive not only in establishing the whereabouts of victims, but also in determining the criminal liability of certain agents of repression. Under Peruvian law, a criminal prosecution can be filed only if: (a) the facts constitute a crime; (b) the case is not subject to the statute of limitations; and (c) the presumptive author is fully identified. Since most military and police agents in the emergency zone act under assumed names, it is difficult to fulfill the last requirement, even if witnesses were to overcome their fear of reprisals and agree to testify. Nonetheless, Escobar has been able to file charges against an officer named Florencio Eguía Dávalos (aka "Butler"), commander of the military post in Cangallo, for his alleged responsibility in nine disappearances. At the time of our visit in July, the Office was preparing a separate action against an Army officer identified in a photograph; his name and rank had been requested from the Joint Command.

Escobar's jurisdiction is limited to the Ayacucho emergency zone, and there only to the investigation of disappearances. The Prosecutor General, however, has twice extended Escobar's mission: first, to investigate disappearances in late 1987 in San Martín Department, and then to look into the massacre of Cayara. At the time of our visit, Escobar had requested an extension of his territorial jurisdiction to permit him to investigate disappearances in Huancavelica and Apurímac, areas which are close to Huanta, as well as in other parts of Ayacucho.

Escobar's accomplishments have been recognized by the human rights community and by the residents of Ayacucho. The Political-Military Command, however, has tried to hinder his work. It has refused to make vehicles and transportation available, ignored written requests for information, and refused to grant him access to facilities. The Ayacucho Office has no vehicles of its own and when Escobar has asked for one from the PIP, the Command has ordered all vehicles to remain in Huamanga. On some occasions, Escobar has used vehicles belonging to the University of San Cristóbal de Huamanga, but University authorities have been pressured to stop this practice.

Since he assumed his duties, Escobar has received several threats to his life. In addition, in August 1987, the military arrested a person who served as Escobar's guide and interpreter in quechua; he was released only two weeks later, after great international pressure.

After the Cayara incidents, the situation in Ayacucho has taken a turn for the worse. Escobar's office has received an increasing number of complaints of disappearances. And, as noted, Escobar was threatened by the Comando Rodrigo Franco in August, only a few days after this new paramilitary group murdered attorney Manuel Febres in Lima and blew up the Ayacucho grave of young *senderista* Edith Lagos. In addition, Escobar has been subjected to the above-mentioned outrageous public attack by Senator Carlos Melgar. Americas Watch urges the government of President Alan García to condemn the attacks on Escobar, to offer him protection and full support in his work, and to disassociate itself categorically from Senator Melgar's attacks.

73

X. THE ROLE OF THE UNITED STATES

The U.S. Department of State has expressed little interest in the situation of human rights in Peru in the last few years. Nonetheless, the Country Reports on Human Rights Practices, which are published yearly by Congressional mandate, have included chapters on Peru that describe the situation accurately and without political or ideological distortions.* It appears that Peru only sporadically raises interest in Washington among either political party, and then only on the subjects of the drug trade, the foreign debt and terrorism, roughly in that order. In our opinion, urgent attention must be paid to two other topics: the stability of Peruvian democracy, and the need to confront political violence while maintaining full respect for human rights.

In the last few months, the United States Embassy in Lima has sponsored exchanges between Peruvian military officers and anti-terrorism experts brought from the United States. As far as we have been able to determine, these have been private but not secret encounters and — up to now — they do not constitute military training. In June 1988 three United States experts held a series of meetings in Peru with Peruvian officers. One expert was an official in the Anti-Terrorism Office of the State Department; one of the other two was César Sereseres of the University of California, who is known for his position in favor of drastic counterinsurgency measures in Guatemala and his defense of the Guatemalan military regimes at the time of widespread massacres and the forced displacement of Indian communities. The State Department official,

---

* See: Human Rights Watch and Lawyers Committee for Human Rights, Critique of the State Department's Country Reports of 1987, New York, 1988. Although several chapters on other countries in the State Department volume include gross distortions dictated by American foreign policy, the chapter on Peru deserves commendation for its objectivity.

whose name was not immediately made known, had been previously stationed in El Salvador.

There have also been news reports that United States advisors assigned to the Embassy's Military Group have been offering advice to their Peruvian colleagues.* In this case, too, the exchange seems to be limited, for the time being, to advice rather than training. Finally, it is widely known that there are United States advisors in the Peruvian jungle, assisting in coca-crop eradication and the struggle against drug trafficking. Drug traffickers share broad sections of the jungle with Sendero Luminoso or the MRTA. Sendero has adopted the strategy of siding with coca growers and leading their struggle. Because security forces thus are obligated to fight against both narcotics dealers and their insurgent allies, the U.S. advisors must find it difficult to remain at arm's length from counter-insurgency operations.

We have no detailed knowledge of the activity of the advisors or of the content of the conversations held by the experts. Nothing of what we have heard, however, indicates that the U.S. representatives are compromising the principle that the struggle against subversion be conducted within the law and in strict compliance with fundamental human rights standards. At the same time, regardless of the content of the advice given, this U.S. presence raises the question of compliance with Section 502B of the Foreign Assistance Act of 1961, as amended (22 USC 2304). That provision prohibits the United States from providing military aid to countries that engage in a "consistent pattern of gross violations of internationally recognized human rights abuse." As this report demonstrates, the armed and security forces of Peru plainly fall within such a category and are therefore undeserving of any aid.

For Fiscal Year 1989, the Reagan Administration has requested moderate sums of aid to Peru, as follows: $15 million in development assistance; $2 million in Economic Support Funds (ESF); $25.9 million in Food for Peace; $10 million in drug enforcement, and $560,000 in military training. There has been no request for aid under the Military Assistance Program (MAP) or for

---

*   Miami Herald, July 5, 1988.

Foreign Military Sales and Credits (FMS). Of these amounts, ESF and military training funds are subject to the restriction of Section 502B and should not be approved. If they are approved, the United States Congress must at once begin oversight activities to find out what, if any, safeguards the Administration is using to ensure compliance with Section 502B.

In our view, the purpose of this legislation is to disassociate the United States from violations that may be committed by friendly governments and forces, and its origin is the disastrous experiences of clandestine and public aid to repressive Latin American military and police forces in the 1960's. The law, however, also plays a constructive role, in that it acts as an incentive for potential recipients to respect human rights as a condition for receiving American aid. The latter depends, of course, on the political will of those who shape or implement United States foreign policy, as well as, in this case, of those who govern Peru.

In recent Latin American experience, U.S. military assistance and the sale of U.S. weapons have created a direct relationship between the Pentagon and the recipient's military establishment. These links can be of decisive importance in determing the fate of the fragile democracies in the hemisphere. For that reason, any contact between the United States and Peruvian officers must take place against the background of a clear position of respect for democratic institutions, including the principle of the authority of elected officials over those who bear arms. In the same sense, those who participate in such contacts must insist that full respect for human rights is the most effective means to fight against terrorism.

This is particularly true in the case of Peru, not only because of the need to confront an increasingly dangerous insurgency, but also because in the last twenty years the Peruvian armed forces have developed without significant contact with their American colleagues (at least relative to the rest of Latin America). On the eve of an imminent increase in those contacts, Americas Watch suggests that the topics outlined in the preceding paragraphs be the subject of a broad debate, both in Lima and in Washington.

XI. RECAPITULATION: WHY ARE HUMAN RIGHTS VIOLATED IN PERU?

This is the fifth report on human rights in Peru by Americas Watch, and we feel it is important to reflect on some of the factors that, in our judgment, account for the continued violation of those rights. The following is not meant as an exhaustive list, but rather as an agenda of ideas to be discussed.

A.   The Split Between State and Society

Since Peru's birth as a nation, there has been a wide gap between the state and the majority of the population. In 1821, the majority did not consciously participate in the construction of the new republic. In the years since, the state has been unable to solve the most basic problems of society or to meet the most basic needs of its people. Nor has the state been able to forge from its multiracial peoples a common identity or a sense of shared culture.

On the contrary, various forces work to perpetuate a fragmented society. For example, members of many Indian communities in the conflict zones adopt an attitude that an anthropologist has called "structural hypocrisy."* When Sendero arrives, they pretend to be pro-Sendero; when the armed forces come, they simulate allegiance to the government. There is a lack of identification with a State that is regarded as a distant stranger. The same lack of identification with one's fellow countryman is at the root of Peruvian racism; although there is no legally ordained segregation, Indians and nonwhites continue to suffer visible exclusion from mainstream society.

This breakdown of the sense of national unity has helped breed an excessive centralism, reinforcing the importance of the capital at the expense of poorer and more remote regions. Power, services and resources are

---

*   Carlos Iván Degregori, "Cultura y Democracia," in Democracia: Realidades y Perspectivas," several authors, Instituto Bartolomé de las Casas, Rimac, Lima, 1988.

disproportionately concentrated in the capital. Although the government of President Alan García has pushed significant legislative initiatives to address the need to decentralize, the results, unfortunately, are so far meager.

This gap between State and society allows us to understand the dramatic surge in violence in recent times, just as it explains its frequent recurrence throughout the history of the Republic. A State that is unable to maintain control through consensus must resort to violence to assert its authority. In turn, this generates a situation in which diverse sectors of society — terrorists, drug traffickers, common criminals — use violence as a way of life, and as the principle medium for addressing the State.

B.   Counter-Insurgency Strategy

Elsewhere in this report we have described the counter-insurgency doctrine that prevails in Peru and its effect on the population of the regions where it is applied. After eight years of frequent human rights violations, it is safe to say that those violations are not exceptions or mistakes, but the products of a systematic, deliberate policy, based on a specific conception of how the war against the insurgents should be fought. This conception has no place for the human rights of either the enemy or the civilian population that lives in the conflict zone. Violations of these rights is seen as a prerequisite to victory, even though such violations have brought victory no closer and, in our view, have served to perpetuate the war.

Although this counter-insurgency strategy has consistently led to disappearances, clandestine common graves and deaths among innocent civilians — yielding a growing national and international outcry — the strategy has undergone no qualitative changes. There has been no real effort to adopt a new strategy which would include the specific directive that the international instruments to which Peru is a party must be honored.

C.   The Attitude of the Insurgent Groups

As stated before, both of the insurgent groups, particularly Sendero Luminoso, engage in a pattern of violations of the laws of war, and their violent actions frequently target innocent civilians. The resort to such methods,

80

particularly when alternative democratic avenues are open, is an act of provocation, designed to elicit a violent response on the part of the State.* Americas Watch condemns these methods in the strongest possible terms.

D.   The Weakness of the Judicial System

As described in the body of this report, the administration of criminal justice in Peru is in the midst of a deep crisis. Courts and procedures are perceived as inefficient and corrupt, and as incapable of confronting the threat posed by insurgent groups. At the same time, the courts are unable to address violations committed by security forces. The jurisdiction of military courts has become little more than an excuse for total impunity for members of military forces. As a result, the Peruvian people have little faith in the judicial institutions, which fail to provide a reasonable alternative to violence for those seeking redress of their grievances. The weakness and incompetence of the judiciary also acts as a convenient ideological pretext for those in the armed and security forces who want to justify resorting to illegal means to attack those considered subversive.

E.   The Lack of Political Will on the Part of Civilian Governments Since 1980

Although security forces are fundamentally responsible for the violations they commit, the two most recent civilian governments have failed to develop the political will to change the attitude of those forces. Of course, fundamental structural problems that generate violence cannot be resolved in one term of government; but a government's decision to end human rights violations can and should be made and implemented within one term, provided the political will to do so exists.

The Belaúnde and García administrations have lacked this political will, the former perhaps more so than the latter. They have failed to impart clear

---

*   Carlos Chipoco, "Violencia y Defensa de la Vida en el Perú," in <u>Revista Latinoamericana de Derechos Humanos</u>, No. 1, Lima, April 1988.

orders to governmental forces to protect citizens, and they have failed to punish violators. With such an attitude, both Presidents have placed the legitimacy of democracy at grave risk, since the system is based on a Constitution that clearly obligates public officials to protect the rights of the governed.

F.   The Lack of Mobilization of the Citizenry

Civil society has to some extent reacted to human rights violations, and its institutions have attempted to generate awareness about them among the population, but these efforts have so far been insufficient to mobilize the Peruvian citizenry to demand an immediate end to such abuses. The Catholic Church has played an outstanding role in combatting human rights abuses, through CEAS's programs in different parts of the country, including the Southern Andes. These programs assist and represent victims, and they promote campaigns in defense of human life. Secular human rights organizations have also played an important role in curbing the wave of violence; they have contributed by clarifying cases of disappeared persons, providing human rights education and information, representing victims of abuses, and pressuring the institutions of the State to live up to their duties and roles under the Constitution.

There have also been efforts by independent groups of citizens to call attention to the need to address human rights violations. A statement entitled *El Quinto: No Matar* ("Fifth Commandment: Thou Shalt Not Kill") was circulated by lay Catholics and signed by hundreds of intellectuals and community leaders. Another statement by prestigious intellectuals of different political persuasions recently called attention to the country's perilous situation and proposed seven basic commitments: to defend life, to affirm democracy, to adapt society to the natural environment, to reconcile political and civil society, to enforce social justice, to affirm the primacy of ethical principles, and to search for a common project.*

---

*   Paid advertisement (no title), El Comercio, August 6, 1988.

The human rights organizations of Peru have joined together in a campaign to put a stop to disappearances, consisting of a variety of actions and statements over several months. All of these efforts are designed to mobilize the citizenry across social and political barriers, towards the common goal of bringing human rights violations to an end. They are all steps in the right direction, which Americas Watch wholeheartedly supports. They also deserve the support of all Peruvians of good will. They are, unfortunately, insufficient at this time. Many more hearts and minds must be won before a national consensus can be developed against violence and in favor of full respect for human rights.

AMERICAS WATCH

☐ REPLY TO: 36 WEST 44TH STREET, NEW YORK, NEW YORK 10036 (212) 840-9460   TELEX 910240 1007 FFFEXPRSN NY

☐ REPLY TO: 739 EIGHTH STREET, S.E., WASHINGTON, D.C. 20003 (202) 546-9336   TELEX 910240 1006 FFEXPRSN

☐ REPLY TO: 234 HOTEL CAMINO REAL, SAN SALVADOR, EL SALVADOR, C.A. (503) 24-5966

Lima, July 11, 1988

His Excellency Alan García Pérez
President of the Republic of Peru
Palacio de Gobierno
Lima

Dear President García,

I write to express our concern about the restrictions recently imposed on our work. As your government was aware, I traveled to the emergency zone of Ayacucho on July 8-9 to learn of the human rights situation there and to investigate violations committed by both sides.

On July 9, police personnel informed me that I needed permission from the Politico-Military Command of Ayacucho in order to carry out my work in the area. I held an interview that morning with army General José Valdivia, chief of that command, who denied me permission to travel to Huanta and told me I must leave the emergency zone. He added that I should have obtained prior permission from the Joint Command of the Armed Forces. As you are aware, in the days before my visit I met with the Minister of the Interior and the Minister of Justice, and in spite of having made clear my interest in visiting Ayacucho, I was never informed that I needed special permission. To the contrary, I was assured of your government's eagerness to allow us to carry out our work throughout the entire territory of Peru.

On the night of July 9, the Politico-Military Command telephoned me to say that after having consulted with the Joint Command in Lima about my situation, it was agreed that I could neither travel in the emergency zone nor carry out any activity in Ayacucho. I returned to Lima on the first flight on Sunday, July 10.

Considering the fact that others, both Peruvians and foreigners, travel to the emergency zone and move around without difficulty, one can only conclude that the restriction imposed on Americas Watch is similar to the impediments placed on the press for several months which we have mentioned in previous reports. As we have stated before, we feel we must insist that free access be permitted the press and human rights groups in the emergency zone.

Last night, during a television program, Senator Carlos Melgar, president of the commission investigating the events in Cayará, offered me the opportunity to return to the zone with parliamentary investigators. I should note that opposition legislators made me a similar offer in Ayacucho on July 9. Americas Watch deeply appreciated Senator Melgar's generous offer; however, as I'm sure you understand, our organization generally declines to participate in official or domestic investigations. We limit ourselves to requesting from authorities in each country we visit permission to conduct our own investigations throughout the country without interference.

Simultaneously, an episode occurred in Ayacucho which Americas Watch considers a serious attack on the human rights movement and which we emphatically protest. I refer to the arbitrary and unjustified detention of four individuals linked to the Comisión Episcopal de Acción Social, an agency of the Catholic Church with which Americas Watch has maintained close relations since 1983. The priest Carlos Gallagher, Pilar Coll, Susana González, and Elsa Ballón were arrested in Ayacucho July 9 and freed late on the night of July 10, without any reason offered that would explain this inadmissable interference in the work of a prestigious organization whose work is recognized throughout our continent. Americas Watch trusts that your government will take the necessary steps to guarantee the work of CEAS in the future and avoid repetition of this unprecedented attack on the human rights movement.

What most seriously concerns Americas Watch, however, is that this interference with human rights work coincides with a notable increase in reports of forced disappearances, particularly in the Huanta area. During my brief stay in Ayacucho, before I was expelled from the zone, I received direct testimony indicating that military forces had detained two eyewitnesses to the Cayará massacre of last May 14. To date these witnesses remain disappeared.

The case is that of Guzmán Bautista Palomino and Gregorio Ipurre Ramos, who were detained in their homes in Cayará in front of witnesses by uniformed men on June 29, just a few meters from the military base established there since the May episodes. Bautista and Ipurre presented testimony of great value to judicial, legislative or journalistic investigations undertaken since the Cayará massacre, which your government has promised to examine. The same night, June 29, Ipurre's parents, Humberto

Ipurre and Benigna Palomino, and his sister, Catalina Ramos Palomino, were also detained. We understand that on July 3, other witnesses from Cayará were detained and later freed, however to the best of our knowledge, the five persons detained on June 29 remain disappeared.

Americas Watch urges your government to undertake energetic measures to bring about the reappearance alive of these five people, and to allow them to freely offer their testimony about the tragic events of Cayará. We also request the President's personal intervention to guarantee the security of the wives of the witnesses, Mrs. Benedicta Tarqui de Bautista and Adelina Tello Palomino de Ipurre.

We trust that you will share our concern about these incidents, and we bring them to your attention so that the appropriate corrective measures will be taken, and especially, so that the integrity of the investigations you have ordered be protected.

I thank you in advance for your attention to these concerns, and take this opportunity to express my best regards.

Juan E. Méndez
Director of Washington
Office
Americas Watch

Recent Publications of the
AMERICAS WATCH

Argentina:
"Truth and Partial Justice in Argentina," August 1987, 88 pages, $6.00, ISBN 0-938579-34-7

Brazil:
"Police Abuses in Brazil," December 1987, 59 pages, $5.00, ISBN 0-938579-40-1

Chile:
"Chile: Human Rights and the Plebiscite," 255 pages, $15.00, ISBN 0-938579-64-9

"The Vicaria de la Solidaridad in Chile," December 1987, 45 pages, $4.00, ISBN 0-938579-39-8

Human Rights Concerns in Chile, March 1987, 53 pages, $4.00

Columbia:
"Human Rights in Columbia as President Barco Begins," September 1986, 68 pages, $7.00, ISBN 0-938579-26-6

Cuba:
"Twenty Years and Forty Days: Life in a Cub an Prison," April 1986, 125 pages, $8.00, ISBN 0-938579-18-5

Ecuador:
"Human Rights in Ecuador," March 1988, 86 pages, $5.00 (Americas Watch/ Andean Commission of Jurists), ISBN 0-938579-59-2

El Salvador:
"Nightmare Revisited 1987-88: Tenth Supplement to the Report on Human Rights in El Salvador, September 1988, 89 pages, $6.00, ISBN 0-929692-03-9

"Labor Rights in El Salvador," March 1988, 119 pages, $8.00, ISBN 0-938579-60-6

"Human Rights in El Salvador on the Eve of the Elections 1988," March 1988, 40 pages, $4.00

Guatemala:
"Human Rights in Guatemala During President Cerezo's First Year," February 1987, 108 pages. $8.00 ISBN 0-938579-31-2

Guyana:
"Political Freedom in Guyana," November 1985, 60 pages, $5.00 (British Parliamentary Human Rights Group/Americas Watch)

Haiti:
"Haiti: Terror and the 1987 Elections, November 1987, 100 pages. $7.00 (Americas Watch/National Coalition for Haitian Refugees)

Honduras:
"The Sumus in Nicaragua and Honduras, An Endangered People," September 1987, 43 pages. $4.00, ISBN 0-938579-36-3

"Human Rights in Honduras: Central America's Sideshow," May 1987, 150 pages, $8.00, ISBN 0-938579-33-9

Jamaica:
"Human Rights in Jamaica," September 1986, 64 pages, $6.00, ISBN 0-938579-27-4

Nicaragua:
"Human Rights in Nicaragua: August 1987 to August 1988," August 1988, 128 pages, $10.00, ISBN 0-929692-01-2

"November 1987 Supplement to the Report on Violations of the Laws of War by Both Sides in Nicaragua," November 1987, 58 pages. $4.00

"The Sumus in Nicaragua and Honduras, An Endangered People," September 1987, 43 pages. $4.00, ISBN 0-938579-36-3

Panama:
"Human Rights in Panama," April 1988, 71 pages, $6.00, ISBN 0-938-579-61-4

Paraguay:
"Human Rights in Paraguay on the Eve of Elections," An Americas Watch Briefing, February 1988, 19 pages

Peru:
"A Certain Passivity, Failing to Curb Human Rights Abuses in Peru," December 1987, 57 pages, $5.00, ISBN 0-938579-31-1

Suriname:
"Human Rights in Suriname," March 30, 1983, 7 pages, $1.00

General
"Annual Report, 1987," January 1988, 41 pages

"Compliance with the Human Rights Provisions of the Central American Peace Plan," August 4, 1988, 8 pages

"Compliance with the Human Rights Provisions of the Central American Peace Plan," January 1988, 47 pages, $4.00

Human Rights Policies:
"The Persecution of Human Rights Monitors in South Africa: June 1988 Supplement to the Worldwide Survey," 38 pages (Human Rights Watch),

"Critique — Review of the Department of State's Country Reports on Human Rights Practices for 1987," June 1988, 192 pages, $12.00 (Human Rights Watch), ISBN 0-938579-63-0

"The Persecution of Human Rights Monitors, December 1986 to December 1987, A Worldwide Survey, December 1987, 107 pages, $7.00 (Human Rights Watch), ISBN 0-938579-44-4

"The Reagan Administration's Record on Human Rights in 1987," December 1987, 210 pages. $12.00 (Lawyers Committee for Human Rights/Human Rights Watch) ISBN 0-938579-42-8

Periodic Newsletters:
"Chile News in Brief," Annual subscription $20.00

"Guatemala News in Brief," Annual subscription $20.00

In this, its fifth report on Peru, Americas Watch concludes that the government of President Alan Garcia has failed, in its three years in office, to affirm democratic authority over the military, leading to no substantial improvement in the human rights situation. Since 1980, when the Maoist extremist group *Sendero Luminoso* (Shining Path) initiated its armed confrontation with the government, political violence has spread throughout the country, claiming thousands of victims.

Among the most serious violations of human rights and the laws of war discussed in this report:
- The military's continuing practice of coerced disappearances, primarily in the Ayacucho emergency zone;
- Army massacres of peasants, particularly in the emergency zone;
- Selective murders by insurgent groups in both the countryside and the cities;
- Torture at the hands of security forces remains a regular method for interrogation of detainees;
- Restrictions on the work of the International Committee of the Red Cross, other humanitarian and human rights organizations and journalists in the Ayacucho emergency region;
- Military jurisdiction continues to be the pretext for the effective impunity enjoyed by all members of the armed forces who commit human rights violations.

In the view of Americas Watch, the Garcia government's tolerance of gross abuses of human rights is more and more apparent. The civilian government must be held accountable for this inaction and complacency, and for its acquiescence in the serious crimes committed by the armed forces in the name of defending the democratic system.

ISBN 0-929692-05-